MW00620904

Teaching Readers
(Not Reading)

Moving Beyond Skills and Strategies
to Reader-Focused Instruction

PETER AFFLERBACH

THE GUILFORD PRESS
New York   London

Copyright © 2022 The Guilford Press
A Division of Guilford Publications, Inc.
370 Seventh Avenue, Suite 1200, New York, NY 10001
www.guilford.com

All rights reserved

Except as indicated, no part of this book may be reproduced, translated, stored in a
retrieval system, or transmitted, in any form or by any means, electronic, mechanical,
photocopying, microfilming, recording, or otherwise, without written permission
from the publisher.

Printed in the United States of America

This book is printed on acid-free paper.

Last digit is print number: 9   8   7   6   5   4   3   2   1

LIMITED DUPLICATION LICENSE

These materials are intended for use only by qualified professionals.

The publisher grants to individual purchasers of this book nonassignable
permission to reproduce all materials for which photocopying permission is
specifically granted in a footnote. This license is limited to you, the individual
purchaser, for personal use or use with students. This license does not grant the
right to reproduce these materials for resale, redistribution, electronic display, or
any other purposes (including but not limited to books, pamphlets, articles, video
or audio recordings, blogs, file-sharing sites, Internet or intranet sites, and handouts
or slides for lectures, workshops, or webinars, whether or not a fee is charged).
Permission to reproduce these materials for these and any other purposes must be
obtained in writing from the Permissions Department of Guilford Publications.

Library of Congress Cataloging-in-Publication Data

Names: Afflerbach, Peter, author.
Title: Teaching readers (not reading) : moving beyond skills and strategies
    to reader-focused instruction / Peter Afflerbach.
Description: New York : The Guilford Press, 2022. | Includes
    bibliographical references and index.
Identifiers: LCCN 2021041729 | ISBN 9781462548613 (paperback) |
    ISBN 9781462548620 (hardcover)
Subjects: LCSH: Reading (Elementary) | Reading (Middle school) | Reading,
    Psychology of. | BISAC: EDUCATION / Teaching Methods & Materials /
    Language Arts | EDUCATION / Secondary
Classification: LCC LB1573 .A36 2022 | DDC 372.4—dc23
LC record available at https://lccn.loc.gov/2021041729

For Jim and Joan

About the Author

Peter Afflerbach, PhD, is Professor of Education at the University of Maryland, College Park. His research interests include individual differences in reading, reading comprehension, and reading assessment. Dr. Afflerbach has served on National Academy of Education and National Academy of Sciences committees related to literacy and is a member of the 2025 Reading Framework Committee of the National Assessment of Educational Progress. He was elected to the International Literacy Association's Reading Hall of Fame in 2009, and he is a Fellow of the American Educational Research Association. Dr. Afflerbach has published in numerous theoretical and practical journals. Prior to his university career, he served as a Chapter 1 remedial reading teacher and as a middle school reading and writing teacher. Dr. Afflerbach can be reached at *afflo@umd.edu.*

Contents

Rethinking

x Contents

Choose

Purchasers of this book can download and print the reproducible appendix
at *www.guilford.com/afflerbach-forms* for personal use or use with students
(see copyright page for details).

Introduction

This book is intended to encourage discussion and action on the essentials of helping student readers grow. In the book, I present the case for *teaching readers* and not teaching reading. Teaching readers involves focusing on all of the factors that influence students' reading growth and achievement beyond cognitive strategies and skills. We have vast knowledge about how children grow as enthusiastic, lifelong readers. However, reading instruction may not regularly reflect this understanding. Powerful influences on students' reading—such as metacognition, motivation and engagement, self-efficacy, and attributions—do not receive appropriate attention in many classrooms. The result is a failure to address all that matters in students' reading development.

We hope that all our students become accomplished readers—individuals who appreciate reading and who read regularly. The beginning readers who thrill to a shared tale, elementary students motivated to act based on their reading about endangered species, adolescents who seek out books related to a pressing life issue, young adults reading as they shape career goals, all who find solace in a story—these are the healthy readers we strive to foster. Being a reader features in their personalities. These students' reading achievement and the path to this achievement represent much more than a collection of reading strategies and skills. As such, *teaching the reader* should be the focus of our instructional efforts.

Teaching readers, as opposed to teaching reading, requires a broad perspective on what developing student readers need, how they thrive, and how our instruction best serves them. In the most successful classrooms, teachers have long understood that effective reading instruction must be partnered with student awareness, enthusiasm, and a belief in self. Teaching readers also addresses the complexity of student readers' development. Teaching readers encourages metacognition and reflection as students become mindful about their reading. It augments students' strategy and skill development, creating high motivation and deep engagement. Teaching readers helps students build self-efficacy as they work through challenging texts and tasks and experience success with reading. And teaching readers helps students develop epistemological knowledge so that they grow with—and through—their interactions with text.

In contrast to teaching readers, *teaching reading* predominates in many classrooms and reflects a strategy and skill approach to instruction. Consider the number of times you have encountered the words *cognition, affect,* and *conation* (or, cognitive, affective, and conative) in your professional readings and discussions. Each word represents factors and influences that are central to human development and human accomplishment, including our students' reading. Yet, too often reading instruction is framed by—and limited to—a cognitive perspective, which leads to teaching reading and not teaching readers. The cognitive aspects of reading are well researched, and they are invaluable for student readers' success. The cognitive focus of much of reading instruction derives from cognitive models of how reading "works": how we decode, how we read fluently, how we learn new vocabulary, and how we comprehend. These models of reading have been divided and subdivided into parts that are amenable to instruction: teaching a comprehension strategy or how to decode consonant blends. A result is that teaching reading involves lessons and units revolving around cognitive strategy and skill. Children learn sound–symbol relationships, increase their fluency, grow their vocabularies, and develop comprehension strategies to identify important information, to predict a story line, and to effectively retell a text. A hoped-for outcome of teaching reading is that these parts sum to comprehensive coverage of what students need to become lifelong readers. The expectation is that strategies and skills fit together to produce accomplished reading, and when this approach is working well, test scores improve. However, cognition is but one factor in reading achievement, and test scores are but one indicator of how student readers develop.

Distinctions between teaching readers and teaching reading are embodied in our responses to the following questions, which reflect the diverse factors that influence students' reading growth:

- Does our instruction help students develop self-awareness so that they can appreciate that their effort influences the outcomes of their reading?
- Are our students encouraged to reflect on how reading works and why reading is important in their lives?
- Do our classrooms support students so that they grow to regard themselves as readers?
- Do our students believe they can succeed at reading?
- Have we helped our students grow so that they choose reading over attractive alternatives?
- Are our students motivated to read frequently and widely?
- Does our teaching result in students who accurately perceive their reading strengths and challenges?
- Do our students grow in the ability to make accurate attributions for performance and growth?

Next, consider these questions related to students who struggle:

- Are our students moving from a general lack of awareness to mindfulness in regard to their reading?
- Are our students evolving from being easily discouraged by reading to being highly motivated to persevere through reading challenges?
- Does our teaching help students progress from avoiding reading at all costs to learning to love reading?
- Are our students learning to make accurate attributions for their reading performance?
- Are our students growing in their appreciation of how reading can be a resource—how it can add to their lives—in and out of school?

When we answer "Yes" to these questions, it reflects our attention to all the important aspects of reading development. We are teaching readers.

Teaching readers helps us address diverse goals and promotes an awareness of opportunities and resources. These issues matter for all developing readers, but especially for those readers who experience difficulty. When we reflect on our students and the positive influences of our teaching, we should look beyond increases in test percentile rankings and changes in students' stanines or raw test scores. We should focus also on the evolving pride in self, a "can-do" attitude, the mindful retellings, the animated discussions, and the demonstration that reading is "working" and is embraced by once-struggling students.

As I note throughout this book, productive discussions about the diverse factors that influence students' reading development never devolve into an either–or debate, as is the case with decades-long and ongoing "reading wars" or with the idea that there is only one exclusionary "science of reading" that should inform our instruction. Students' self-efficacy when trying to comprehend a challenging text is as important as using phonics to unlock the meaning of a printed word. And learning and using vocabulary are as important as making appropriate attributions for one's reading performance. It is time to focus on *all* of the factors that influence reading development, to examine their power, to understand their relationships, and to realize their promise in nurturing accomplished and enthusiastic student readers. It is time for teaching readers.

PLAN OF THE BOOK

In the five chapters of Part I, Teaching Reading or Teaching Readers?: Moving Beyond a Focus on Strategies and Skills, I go beyond the traditional strategy and skill focus of teaching reading to set the stage for teaching readers. I ask readers of this book to partake of a reading experience that illustrates the diverse factors that influence reading. The experience also helps us appreciate the strategies we use as readers. I next define and describe concepts that help me build my argument for teaching readers. They involve the consideration of students' metacognition and mindfulness, self-efficacy, motivation and engagement, and attributions and epistemic beliefs. Then I trace the history of reading research and classroom practice and describe how the reading instruction focus has narrowed, privileging skill and strategy, while often excluding other integral factors in students' reading development.

In Part II, Teaching Readers: Examining the Factors That Influence Reading Development and Reading Achievement, I introduce and devote separate chapters to each factor: metacognition and mindfulness, self-efficacy, motivation and engagement, attributions, and epistemic beliefs. I provide a general overview of each factor, accompanied by research that demonstrates the power of the factor in students' reading. I describe how each one may act to support or impede reading development, and

I describe classroom contexts that support such growth. These contexts consist of intellectual, social, and physical spaces, and classroom vignettes are used to highlight and describe the broad-based nature of student readers' growth and how to positively influence that development. I also focus on the powerful interactions that take place between these factors to influence students' daily reading and their long-term reading development. I conclude each chapter with an examination of assessments that are designed to chart student growth related to the broad outcomes of teaching readers beyond omnipresent strategy and skill quizzes and tests or comprehension questions. We are fortunate that the constructs related to readers' metacognition, conation, affect, attributions, and epistemologies are well defined. This affords us the opportunity to contemplate assessments that chart student development in relation to these diverse constructs.

The book concludes with an Appendix, the Healthy Readers Profile, for constructing accounts of readers' development. My intent with this tool is to suggest how teachers can gather the information that helps them best understand students' broad reading development. The Healthy Readers Profile can also help teachers plan instruction and support. The Profile is also intended to help teachers and schools provide a broadened account—beyond strategy and skill growth—of the array of positive outcomes of teaching readers.

This book does not provide details on teaching reading strategies or building reading skills, as there are many excellent resources that do so. Rather, the book is intended as a necessary counterpart, and alternative account, to detailed descriptions of students' reading development and related instruction.

TEACHING READING OR TEACHING READERS?
Moving Beyond a Focus on Strategies and Skills

Reading = Strategy + Skill

Readers = Complete portrait of reader
theory, practice Research

This book explains critical differences between teaching reading and teaching readers. Whereas teaching reading focuses on delivering strategy and skill instruction, teaching readers operates from a broader base of theory, research, and practice. Teaching readers helps us focus on a more complete portrait of the student as reader. Part I begins with an introduction to the rationale for the book, along with an overview of the sciences of reading, accompanied by research that supports a comprehensive approach to teaching our student readers. I next ask users of this book to examine our own reading ability as we are challenged by a difficult paragraph. This experience is intended to illustrate the diverse factors beyond strategy and skill that operate during reading. The next chapter introduces key terms and their definitions that are encountered in the subsequent chapters of the book. I follow this chapter with an account of 100 years of research that describes students' reading development and reading achievement and that asks the question, "Is teaching strategies and skills enough?" Finally, I explain why the vast majority of reading instruction has a singular focus on cognitive strategies and skills. I cite the prevalence of testing to assess the cognitive aspects of reading, biased media accounts of why some children do not learn to read, and the misguided notion that there is a single "science of reading" as major forces in maintaining the strategy and skill instruction status quo.

CHAPTER 1

Why Teaching Readers
Is Different from Teaching Reading

Research demonstrates that student readers' growth is influenced by an array of cognitive, metacognitive, affective, conative, and epistemic factors (Pearson, Palincsar, Biancarosa, & Berman, 2020). Accordingly, they should each be a focus of reading curriculum and instruction. This is not an either–or proposition—we cannot attend to one at the expense of another, and we cannot rank order their importance. We must use our expanding, detailed knowledge of human development and reading development to shape instruction for teaching readers. When we teach readers (as opposed to teaching reading), we can focus on the range of factors that influence reading growth. In fact, as we help students develop the strategies and skills that will serve them throughout their lives as readers, we can connect this learning with such critical areas as metacognition, self-efficacy, mindfulness, and motivation and engagement.

All students benefit from a broad conceptualization of what matters in becoming successful readers (Afflerbach, Cho, Kim, Crassas, & Doyle, 2013). The students who most need improvement in self-efficacy, who need positive motivation, engagement, enhanced reflection, and metacognition, are quite often our struggling readers. Our instruction must focus on these diverse student needs and learning outcomes, as students undertake acts of reading. However, the attention we give to struggling readers should not be interpreted as a "hands-off" message related to our more successful student readers. The continued development of accomplished student readers is just as important as the progress we seek for our struggling students. A student who devours stories may need support to develop self-efficacy when reading history and science texts in fourth grade because self-efficacy is situational. In addition, the ongoing development of metacognition is critical for all students as they work independently with increasingly complex disciplinary texts, multimodal texts, reading on the Internet, and reading-related tasks.

In the following chapters, we will examine singly the factors that influence the course of students' reading development. I note that these factors are marked by interactions and interdependencies. For example, students who are metacognitive and self-aware are better able to identify, understand, and appreciate the relationship between their efforts and the outcomes of their reading. This awareness helps students build self-efficacy and agency and make accurate attributions for their reading performance, which in turn can motivate them to return to reading because they associate reading with success, positive feelings, and being "in control" of their world. One result is a beneficial cascade effect, in which improvements in one aspect of student reading flow into other areas and contribute to overall development.

This book focuses on the positive outcomes of teaching readers. We hope for these outcomes for each and every reader. However, we must acknowledge the challenges that some readers face. Struggling readers have their own sets of individual challenges, and they are often marked by dysfunctional interactions and interdependencies. A reader's low self-efficacy can lead to poor motivation, contributing to less actual reading, which prevents cognitive strategies and skills practice and the development of metacognition. Negative results follow and accumulate. Many student readers who struggle associate their past reading experiences with failure and unhappiness, a negative outcome that contributes to a lack of motivation and engagement with present and future reading. Detachment from reading, an inability to monitor their reading efforts, and a lack of self-awareness can lead these students to make erroneous attributions for their performance. For example, students believing that they are unlucky when they read, and not believing that their effort and attention can influence their work, avoid reading. The related poor motivation leads students away from, instead of toward, reading. I examine various means of reorienting these students to motivation, engagement, and self-efficacy. When teaching readers, we want to take advantage of the interrelated nature of the factors that influence students' reading development and build on positive experiences.

Beneficial Cascade [handwritten marginal note]

These influencers of student development—including metacognition, motivation and engagement, and self-efficacy—assume different roles in reading. They can be, simultaneously, both the conditions for, and the results of, reading. For example, motivation must be present for reading success as students begin a challenging text. And motivation can also be a result of an act of reading, based on the pride a student feels for a job well done with that challenging text, and the realization that reading opens doors to fascinating worlds. A series of successful or unsuccessful reading experiences produces positive or negative motivation, respectively. Positive self-efficacy can lead students to read more, with subsequent success reinforcing that habit. Negative self-efficacy leads students to steer clear of reading. Sufficient prior knowledge is necessary for a student to construct meaning from text, and gains in knowledge are a hoped-for result of reading done well.

Such influences on reading are dynamic, and they can change. A student's generally positive motivation to read can be worn down by a series of unrewarding, or failing, acts of reading. Likewise, a student's low self-efficacy for reading can change through a series of positive experiences that highlight student effort and result in success. The array of factors that influences reading is complex. Teaching in reference to them is challenging. However, the interrelationships of these factors suggest that we can help move students toward successful reading experiences and positive self-images as readers by taking strategic advantages of these relationships.

Keeping track of (let alone addressing and teaching to) the diverse individual differences in our students' reading development can be a monumental task, especially when we consider our already demanding instructional days. How can we find time to attend to motivation, self-efficacy, and metacognition when some of our students struggle to learn sound–symbol correspondences and reading comprehension strategies, and the curricular remedy is limited to repeating the instruction? How can we further contribute to accomplished student reader growth when we are hard-pressed to cover the content in content area reading? From one perspective—one that I encourage throughout this book—the positive interactions of factors like motivation and self-efficacy can support growth and create a synergy for our student readers. This outcome is a valuable return on our investment of teaching time and effort. Students who experience success are in a good position to appreciate and grow in relation to the myriad factors that contribute to their reading growth.

(CHAPTER REVIEW)

1. Describe how teaching readers differs from teaching reading.
2. What are the limitations of teaching only reading strategies and skills?
3. Describe one area of students' reading development that is not always addressed in reading programs.
4. Explain how one factor in reading development (e.g., motivation) can influence another factor (e.g., self-efficacy).
5. What is a possible benefit of teaching both strategies and skills and the factors sketched in this chapter?

1) <u>READers</u> vs <u>Reading</u>

cognitive

- meta cog
- Self awareness
- motivation
- enthusiasm
- self-efficacy

- decoding
- fluency
- vocaB
- comprehension

2) Negative cascade (vs beneficial Cascade)

3) metacog / motivation tc

4) Cascade effect

5) Synergy B/t 2

CHAPTER 2

Experiencing Cognition, Affect, and Conation in Our Reading

In this chapter, I want to examine with you an act of reading—in this case, reading a single paragraph. My hope is that your reading of the paragraph will provide insights into the array of cognitive, metacognitive, affective, conative, and epistemic factors that operate during reading and influence reading.

First, some background: In the 1980s (or, as my daughters say, "ancient history"), I was interested in researching expert readers' cognitive strategies. As a reading researcher, my belief was that if we could describe in sufficient detail the strategies used by accomplished readers, we could then create detailed models of these strategies, such as prediction and summarization. We could then use these models to develop effective reading strategy instruction (Afflerbach, 1990; Johnston & Afflerbach, 1985). Part of my approach to this research involved having expert readers read challenging texts and think aloud as they reported their strategies (Afflerbach & Johnston, 1984). The idea was that a challenging text might de-automatize many of the expert readers' strategies. In turn, this would permit the expert readers to be aware of their strategies, and report on them through thinking aloud. Then, the strategies that experts repeatedly reported (and that were helpful to constructing meaning) could be transformed into cognitive strategy instruction as part of an effective reading program.

To make the expert readers' task sufficiently difficult, I managed to find and then modify texts from academic journals that presented distinct reading challenges. These texts represented a high degree of difficulty, and they demanded expert strategy use. The texts also raised to consciousness the strategies experts used to try to construct meaning and allowed them to report on the strategies. To demonstrate how this exercise works, I would like you to read one such text—let's call it the *broadpoint* paragraph. Your task is to try to comprehend the paragraph. As you read it, make sure to write down or take a mental note of the strategies you are using to try to construct meaning. Please give this your best effort, as the insights you gain from this reading exercise will be called upon throughout this book! Here's the paragraph. Take your time and remember to take note of the strategies you are using.

> *It is legitimate to further characterize the broadpoint appearance as a major archeological horizon marker for the eastern seaboard. In the terms of Willey and Phillips, a horizon is "a primarily spatial continuity represented by cultural traits and assemblages whose nature and mode of occurrence permit the assumption of a broad and rapid spread." That a quick expansion of the broadpoint-using peoples took place is indicated by the narrow range of available radiocarbon dates, along with a correspondingly wide areal distribution of components. Once established, the broadpoint horizon developed as a "whole cultural pattern or tradition" in its own right by persisting and evolving over an expansive region for 500 to 1,000 years.*

What strategies did you use to try to construct meaning? What did you find yourself doing as you read this paragraph? In my research and work with teachers across 4 decades, thousands of expert readers have read this paragraph. These prior readers report using a consistent and predictable core of reading strategies for the *broadpoint* paragraph. I trust that you will find the strategies you used in the following list.

Cognitive Reading Strategies

- Scanning and skimming the text to "size up" the task at hand
- Accessing relevant prior knowledge, if available
- Making near and far inferences
- Assigning importance to words and phrases
- Predicting text contents
- Focusing on vocabulary (e.g., *horizon, broadpoint, radiocarbon dates*) to determine if there is any related prior knowledge
- Visualizing text contents
- Using context to determine the meaning of words and phrases
- Parsing text into shorter, more manageable segments or chunks of text

* Paraphrasing and translating sections of the text into more familiar terms
* Summarizing

I present this list of cognitive reading strategies for several reasons. First, I would like you to feel a kinship with other accomplished readers who gave their best to try to construct meaning for this broadpoint paragraph! No doubt you used some (or all) of the strategies contained in this list. Second, I believe that experts' reports provide strong evidence of the importance of strategies in constructing meaning from text. Strategies clearly play a central role in the reading enterprise. Instruction that helps make these powerful but invisible tools tangible for student readers is critical for reading development. Third, successful readers use these strategies repeatedly. Strategies are keys for trying to unlock the meaning of the unfamiliar material in this challenging text.

Expert readers also report using metacognitive strategies as they try to construct meaning for this challenging paragraph. In fact, a significant proportion of accomplished readers' think-alouds focuses on metacognition, as we might expect when a challenging text is encountered. These reported metacognitive strategies include:

* Setting a goal for reading
* Checking on progress toward the goal
* Noting the lack of relevant prior knowledge for the text topic
* Adjusting the goal
* Noting that the text is difficult
* Predicting the anticipated degree of success
* Stopping reading to check on comprehension
* Detecting a problem
* Slowing down the rate of reading
* Rereading to clarify or establish understanding
* Acknowledging a diminished degree of success

Determining that there is a problem while constructing meaning, identifying the problem (or problems), rereading, slowing the rate of reading, and monitoring progress toward goals are all dependent on readers reflecting and being metacognitive. Overall, think-aloud reporting from expert readers leads me to conclude that they share strategic approaches to reading as well as the specific strategies themselves. The cognitive and metacognitive strategies reported by expert readers are critical for expert readers' attempts to construct meaning.

In asking thousands of accomplished readers to provide reports of their cognitive strategies as they read the broadpoint paragraph, I've inevitably found that these reports include comments related to the readers' affect, conation, epistemic beliefs, and attributions. Consider the following list of "what else" has been reported by the many accomplished readers of the paragraph, *even though the readers were not requested to report their feelings and emotions, motivation and engagement, self-efficacy, attributions, or epistemic knowledge.* In addition to the cognitive strategies they used, expert readers also report:

- Initial high motivation because of the apparently challenging nature of the reading and readers' belief that they will succeed
- Related initial high engagement with the task to prove one's self as an accomplished reader, followed by waning engagement
- Frustration with the inability to understand the text
- Feeling of failure
- Questioning of one's reading ability
- Approaching the reading task with confidence, based on high self-efficacy
- Diminished self-efficacy as reading grinds to a halt
- Self-efficacy challenged near term, but intact long term
- Self-esteem intact due to the realization that this is a purposely difficult text and a belief in the self as strong reader
- Accurate attribution for reading performance focused on the unfamiliarity of the text topic
- Inaccurate attribution for reading performance focused on self-doubt as a reader
- Determination that the best outcome would be a literal understanding of the text and not a critical or evaluative understanding
- Inability to critically evaluate text due to a lack of domain-related prior knowledge
- Discomfort due to an inability to judge the truthfulness of the author
- Discomfort due to an inability to judge the reliability or accuracy of the information in the text
- Quitting the task because it is judged to be not that important
- Conceding to the challenging text because it is seen as purposefully difficult
- Annoyance with the task and with the person who requested participation in performing the task!

Why do expert readers' verbal reports reveal the presence and influence of motivation, self-efficacy, mindfulness, attributions, and the like? Why are these comments included in readers' think-alouds, even when they are not requested? My contention is that these comments and observations "show up" because they reflect important aspects of reading that are always present and always operating. They are an integral part of the reading process, and part of every reader's—even expert readers'—experience. Positive or negative emotion, a willingness to continue, giving effort, pulling back on this effort, bringing a "can-do" attitude (and then having that attitude change), monitoring performance, and "throwing in the towel" are part and parcel of particular acts of reading. That accomplished readers report these "other" aspects of reading—when not asked to do so—affirms their presence and hints at their power. Unfortunately, these influences, which are necessary for reading growth and reading achievement, are not always given appropriate attention in school reading programs.

I hope that this paragraph-reading exercise and explanation provides sufficient evidence to support the claim that while reading strategies and skills are important, they are not all that matters in reading. They are not all that student readers need to succeed at reading. Woven into students' reading growth are threads—cognitive, metacognitive, affective, conative, attributional, and epistemic—and all are intertwined. Like strategies and skills, these critical aspects of reading influence (and are influenced by) students' reading experiences. They are all involved in our students' reading development and reading achievement, and all of them merit our attention as we are teaching readers.

A note: A *broadpoint* is a type of Native American arrowhead. If so inclined, you can reread the paragraph with this single piece of key information to observe how this bit of prior knowledge can greatly influence your construction of meaning!

ACKNOWLEDGING THE PRIVILEGE
OF BEING A SUCCESSFUL ADULT READER

Note that as accomplished adult readers we are in a different position than many of our student readers. Along with the responsibilities of being adults, we also have privileges. We can, more often than not, avoid situations in which we don't believe we will succeed. We can pick and choose the situations and contexts in which we perform publicly. We can decline an invitation to participate in a particular sport if we think we will look foolish. We can avoid a conversation in which our lack of understanding of the topic might quickly become apparent. We can choose the things we want to read, as well as the purposes for our reading. As accomplished readers, our egos, our self-efficacy, and our belief in ourselves are well established, and we protect them. They are not prone to a consequential, long-lasting, and negative reaction due to a single reading of the difficult broadpoint paragraph. We have all had countless successful experiences with our reading, and they protect us from the occasional challenge to our accomplished reader persona. Further, as volunteers to the broadpoint reading task, we can bow out when we want to. We come to and leave the task with our strategies, self-efficacy, and metacognition intact and operating. We believe in ourselves as readers, and we remain motivated readers.

Our students, however, have different realities. They may have histories of reading challenges and failures, and their reading struggles may be more often public than private. Participation in school reading is mandatory, not optional. Demonstrating understanding is required, not suggested. Much of what is read in school is assigned, and the purposes for reading are predetermined and often narrow. Imagine if many of your school reading experiences were similar to the experience of reading the broadpoint paragraph. How often would you seek out reading? How often would you approach reading with enthusiasm? Would you choose reading over more attractive and less threatening alternatives? Would you believe strongly in yourself as a successful reader and anticipate success with each and every reading outcome?

Although affect and conation are not featured in many approaches to reading instruction, we don't need to search far for examples of their power and influence. For me, strong positive feelings for getting together with friends, reading a good book and discussing it, laughing, drinking wine, throwing a Frisbee, and hiking draw me to situations in which either affect or conation is present. I look forward to these people, these places, these activities, and these events. They always draw me back. In contrast, my experiences with visits to the Department of Motor Vehicles have created negative feelings that lead me to try to avoid any in-person visit. My past visits to the DMV in New York, Georgia, Maryland, and California include the following experiences:

- Upon entering, try to make sense of signs that are confusing
- Wait on the first line to be told what line to go to next
- Wait on the second line

- Finally get to the counter to be told that I have the incorrect form or that I've filled it out incorrectly
- Leave the counter without successfully addressing the motor vehicle issue
- Get the correct form
- Wait on the third line

I have analyzed my feelings about the DMV to better understand my wanting to avoid a visit at all costs. Why is the DMV the last place I want to be? It comes down to not feeling in control—in effect, feeling powerless. I expect that I can't get things right, regardless of what I do. Upon entering the DMV office, I do not have any sense that I am in control of my destiny (or even the next step in the process), and these feelings and beliefs arouse negative emotions, which in turn provide a strong motivation to avoid such situations. My history at the DMV includes spending considerable amounts of time trying hard to achieve the goals of my visit, with mixed and unpredictable results. Might conation and affect—my emotions, feelings, and belief that I am not in control of the situation there—be similar to what struggling students feel when they enter their reading classroom? If I had been quickly successful in my previous visits to the DMV, would I have a different perspective on an upcoming visit?

To summarize, reading is a complex mix of cognition, metacognition, affect, and conation. Many factors operate before, during, and after reading to draw students in or to distance them. Our students approach reading with histories of success or failure, and this influences the profile and personality of the reader. Teaching readers allows us to attend to all the factors that influence students' reading development and reading achievement. Teaching readers can help us help our students to maintain histories of success and to transform histories of failure.

Following this brief consideration of the diverse factors that are operating when we read, I'd like to try a thought experiment. The goal of the experiment is to help us try to move closer to the mindset of the challenged reader. This is worth doing because we have experienced success with reading, and we consider ourselves to be (at least) competent readers. Our struggling student readers do not share this mindset, and being sensitive to it is a key to effective instruction. This thought experiment focuses on the array of factors that surround all human activity and our students' reading. I'd like to ask these questions: "Is reading strategy and skill instruction all that our students need to become successful, enthusiastic, and independent readers?" and "Why?"

(CHAPTER REVIEW)

1. What strategies did you use as you attempted to construct meaning for the broadpoint paragraph?

2. What else did you experience as you tried to understand the broadpoint paragraph?

3. What did you learn about your own reading as a result of trying to understand the broadpoint paragraph?

4. What can you bring to your teaching of readers based on your experience in reading the broadpoint paragraph?

5. How did a lack of background knowledge influence your reading of the broadpoint paragraph?

CHAPTER 3

Critical Concepts
Definitions and Descriptions

Four decades as a teacher and researcher have taught me that words really do matter. I have learned that the meaning of a particular word varies based on who is using it and the situation in which it is used. I have learned that one term may be used to describe different concepts, and many terms may be used to describe the same concept. With these thoughts in mind, I'm providing an overview of several key concepts used in this book. I describe and define the terms that are used to represent ideas and practices that contribute to teaching readers. These words and terms represent potentially powerful influences on reading and reading development. In subsequent chapters, we will revisit them; however, here I want to sketch my understanding of these concepts and related terms, as there is not always universal agreement about a single definition.

KEY CONCEPTS USED IN THIS BOOK

Cognition

Cognition includes all conscious and unconscious processes by which knowledge is accumulated, such as perceiving, recognizing, conceiving, and reasoning. Put differently, cognition is a state or experience of knowing that can be distinguished from an experience of feeling or willing. (*www.britannica.com/topic/cognition-thought-process*)

As applied to reading, cognition relates to the strategies, skills, and knowledge that students bring to acts of reading and that permit students' processing, learning, and remembering text. The knowledge that we gain or learn from reading is also an aspect of cognition as well.

Cognitive Strategies and Skills

Cognitive strategies and skills are used by readers to construct meaning from text. Reading skills are automatic and reading strategies are intentional and effortful. (Afflerbach, Pearson, & Paris, 2008, p. 365)

In relation to reading, cognitive strategies and skills are used by readers to decode words, make inferences, link text contents to existing knowledge, determine the meaning of vocabulary, construct understanding, evaluate claims, synthesize across texts, and apply what is learned. Cognitive strategies and skills are the primary focus of the vast amount of current reading instruction.

Affect

[Affect is] a feeling or emotion as distinguished from cognition, thought, or action. Affect refers to the emotional interpretation of perceptions, information, or knowledge. It is generally associated with one's attachment (positive or negative) to people, objects, ideas, etc., and asks the question "How do I feel about this knowledge or information?" (*www.edpsycinteractive.org/topics/affect/affsys. html*)

In relation to reading, affect refers to the feelings and emotions a reader has about reading. Readers can be emotionally engaged or disengaged. A positive affect for reading leads students to read, and a negative affect steers students away from reading.

Conation

[Conation is] an inclination . . . to act purposefully. (*www.merriam-webster.com/dictionary/conation*)

Conation leads student readers to act with purpose. As applied to reading, conation represents the connection of the student's knowledge and affect to reading behavior. Conation is intentional and goal oriented in relation to motivation. Conation fuels students' willful reading efforts. A lack of conation may result in students' failure to give effort and in disengagement with reading.

Mindfulness

[Mindfulness is] maintaining a state of heightened or complete awareness of one's thoughts, emotions, or experiences on a moment-to-moment basis.
(*www.merriamwebster.com/dictionary/mindfulness*)

Mindful student readers are aware of their reading abilities, their reading achievements, their areas of strength and challenge, and the role that reading plays in their lives. Further, mindfulness helps student readers understand, connect, and appreciate the different components of successful reading. This awareness contributes to efficiency in metacognition in reading and in an appreciation of reading accomplishments.

Metacognition

[Metacognition is] an awareness or analysis of one's own learning or thinking processes.
(*www.merriamwebster.com/dictionary/metacognition*)

With respect to reading, metacognition represents the mindsets and strategies that readers use to manage acts of reading—from onset to completion. Metacognition allows students to set goals, monitor comprehension, recognize and fix problems when they are encountered, gauge progress at reading, and determine if goals are met.

Executive Function

[Executive function refers to] the mental processes that enable (readers) to plan, focus attention, remember instructions, and juggle multiple tasks successfully . . . to filter distractions, prioritize tasks, set and achieve goals, and control impulses. (*https://developingchild.harvard.edu/science/key-concepts/executive-function*)

Related to reading, executive function describes students' control of both the acts of reading and the context of reading, how reading is managed, how it is judged to be successful, and how reading "fits" with related reading tasks and responsibilities.

Self-Efficacy

> [Self-efficacy is] the power to produce an effect.
> (*www.merriam-webster.com/dictionary/efficacy*)

Bandura (2006) notes:

> Among the mechanisms of human agency, none is more central or pervasive than belief of personal efficacy. Unless people believe they can produce desired effects by their actions, they have little incentive to act or to persevere in the face of difficulties. (p. 165)

Related to reading, self-efficacy represents students' beliefs about if and how they will be successful in reading. Human beings tend to return to pursuits at which they are successful and to avoid those at which they fail. Our students do the same, and successful readers develop positive self-efficacy and a belief in themselves as readers.

Motivation

> [Motivation is] the act or process of motivating; a motivating force, stimulus, or influence.
> (*www.merriam-webster.com/dictionary/motivation*)

Motivation is a driver of human action. In relation to reading, positive motivation leads students to engage in, persist at, and complete acts of reading, while a lack of motivation leads students away from reading.

Engagement

> [Engagement is] the state of being engaged; emotional involvement or commitment.
> (*www.merriam-webster.com/dictionary/engagement*)

Engagement is often considered the positive outcome of combining motivation and reading goals with strategies and skills. Engagement describes the state of students who are invested in reading, who give full attention to reading, and whose reading is marked by enthusiasm and forbearance. These readers combine positive motivation with their thinking and strategy and skill use.

Epistemic Beliefs and Epistemology

> [Epistemic beliefs are] a person's beliefs about the nature of human knowledge, like its certainty and how it is conceptualized, and a person's beliefs about the criteria for and the process of knowing. (Kienhues, Ferguson, & Stahl, 2016, p. 320)

> [Epistemology is] the philosophical study of the nature, origin, and limits of human knowledge.
> (*www.britannica.com/topic/epistemology*)

With respect to reading, epistemology describes students' understanding of the nature of knowledge contained in texts and students' rights and privileges as readers related to the particular type of knowledge and information in texts—including factual accounts, truths, propaganda, and lies. Early readers often believe everything that appears in print, while more accomplished readers understand that texts may vary in accuracy and truthfulness. Epistemic beliefs underlie this understanding.

Attributions

> [Attribution is] the interpretive process by which people make judgments about the causes of their own behavior.
> (*www.merriam-webster.com/dictionary/attribution*)

Attributions are a self-narrative that an individual creates to explain successes and failures. In relation to reading, attributions are the causes that students assign to reading outcomes. Students can attribute their reading success or challenge to luck, effort, or intelligence—"I have good luck (or don't), I worked hard (or didn't), or I'm smart (or not)," respectively. Attributions—accurate or inaccurate—act as powerful influences on student motivation and self-efficacy.

These words, terms, and definitions are revisited as I progress through the chapters of this book.

(CHAPTER REVIEW)

1. Describe *conation* and how it can influence acts of student reading.
2. Describe *affect* and how it can influence acts of student reading.
3. Describe metacognition, self-efficacy, motivation and engagement, attributions, and epistemic knowledge.
4. Explain how one of these concepts (metacognition, self-efficacy, motivation and engagement, attributions, or epistemic knowledge) operates when students read.
5. Explain how one of these concepts (metacognition, self-efficacy, motivation and engagement, attributions, or epistemic knowledge) might complement a student's use of strategies and skills.

(CHAPTER 4)

Teaching Readers
A History of Knowing Better Than We Are Doing

In this chapter I provide a brief history of how students' reading development has been conceptualized through the lenses of research and education policy. I also describe how this history influences present-day practices of teaching reading and not teaching readers. It's a description of how we have come to understand reading and an explanation of why certain practices still prevail in reading instruction. I am especially interested in the differential attention given to the factors—including motivation, self-efficacy, and strategies and skills—that demonstrably impact our students' reading development. I also point out that although prior generations of teachers and researchers acknowledged the wide range of factors that influence reading development, cognitive strategies and skills are the exclusive focus of many current reading programs. I examine the strong, habitual forces that contribute to strategies and skills being considered the "must haves" of reading and to maintaining the status quo of teaching reading and not teaching readers. Understanding these forces can help us work to change our reading instruction. I believe it is of utmost importance to understand that a lack of attention to teaching readers is not for want of research, theory, or an understanding of the elements of high-quality instruction or of the characteristics of successful classrooms. Rather, it is due to habits, traditions, and societal forces.

A BRIEF HISTORY OF PERSPECTIVES
ON STUDENT READERS AND THEIR DEVELOPMENT

Across a century of reading research, we have learned that students' reading development is influenced by many factors. We might assume that reading instruction would be informed by this understanding, which is based on a strong and broad research foundation. In this chapter I observe that the foundation for much of today's reading instruction is actually narrow, and not broad. Describing this state of affairs is critical for understanding the instructional status quo, which maintains a hyperfocus on cognitive aspects of students' reading development. It can also inform our efforts to change the nature of reading instruction—what we do in our classrooms.

We've known for quite some time that students' reading success depends on more than strategies and skills. In fact, readers' development must be conceptualized as broad based if we hope to teach readers: students who enjoy reading, who view reading as a valuable tool, and who identify as readers. What follows is a brief historical overview of reading research and theory, intended to illustrate what we've learned about reading development. I describe as well the selective attention given to particular aspects of students' reading development and achievement.

The wide range of factors that influence reader development has been documented across the history of reading research. Moore (1938) identified a variety of influences, beyond strategy and skill, that influence young students' readiness for reading:

> Readiness involves many different factors in which a typical pupil is unevenly advanced. At the present time we do not know what weight to give to each and every characteristic. There are certain causes which have received less attention than they seem to deserve. These causes briefly are variation (1) in intelligence, (2) in sensory equipment, (3) in physical equipment, (4) in language ability, (5) in rate of learning, (6) in response to motivation, (7) in sex, and (8) in emotional control. (p. 164)

Moore observes that "we do not know what weight to give to each" factor. This weighting challenge persists today, as indicated by the uneven attention to all the factors involved in reading development. For example, is a student's decoding ability as important, less important, or more important than that student's motivation and engagement with reading? Is a student's high self-efficacy as important, less important, or more important than the ability to read fluently? Based on our answers to these questions, what "weight"—indicated by our instructional focus and class time spent—should be given to each factor? I don't consider asking these questions an idle academic exercise; it reflects the fact that teaching readers means attending to all of the factors that influence reading development. Thoughtful consideration of such questions should result in reading instruction that acknowledges and suitably "weights" all contributors to student growth. Determining the correct balance or weight that should be given to all of students' developmental needs is an ongoing challenge. A theory about how these factors contribute to reading development and how they are addressed through our teaching is critical.

In addition to wanting to determine the appropriate attention to be given to each influence on students' reading development, Moore (1938) noted that some "have received less attention than they seem to deserve." Moore's concern that instruction ignored important aspects of student growth remains valid today. He reasoned that it is important to use a theory of the specifics of students' reading development to guide classroom instruction: "Few of us have a definite guiding philosophy as to what should be our attitude towards the differences we know to exist" (p. 165).

An examination of today's reading programs reveals an emphasis on what Moore termed "language ability" and "rate of learning," represented by strategy and skill instruction in relation to scope and sequence charts. In contrast, "response to motivation" and "emotional control" have been assigned secondary status and are addressed mainly through teacher prerogative.

[handwritten margin note: what we do + don't do]

Decades after Moore's observations, Strang (1961) noted that both nature and nurture, as well as the interaction between them, impact how students develop. Further, she suggested that diverse factors influence both single acts of reading, such as a third-grade student reading a science article on the life cycle of a butterfly, and student's overall reading development, for example, the growth demonstrated across the entire school year at the end of third grade. Here is Strang's perspective on the factors affecting students' reading performance and reading growth:

> Getting meaning from the printed page is a biopsychological process that is influenced by the individual's ability, experiences, needs, attitudes, values, and self-concept. Each individual interacts with the total reading situation in accord with his unique pattern of characteristics. (The reader's) memory of each experience with

> reading further influences the reader's perception of, and response
> to, each new situation. (Strang, 1961, p. 414)

Note that Strang's seemingly contemporary insights were provided more
than 60 years ago. A further critical point here is that students' memories of past reading experiences influence current and future reading
acts. What accumulated knowledge of reading might a student possess?
Memories of success at reading arouse feelings of accomplishment, happiness, and self-worth. These feelings steer a reader toward further reading. The struggling student reader remembers the lack of success, and
perhaps a series of embarrassments, which contribute to diminished self-
confidence and frustration and steer a student away from reading.

Strang (1961) acknowledged the power of affect and conation and
how they further influence students' reading behaviors and development. She maintained that classroom environments—involving teachers,
instruction, texts, tasks, and student groupings—play a significant role
in how student readers develop: "We recognize that the individual does
not learn in isolation but is influenced by the complex social network in
which he lives and learns" (p. 414).

Our attention to both classroom learning environments and students' social networks is necessary for teaching readers. Do students have
the opportunity to discuss and collaborate on reading-related projects
and performances? What are the optimal groupings that help students
meet their goals? Attention to these concerns allows us to address the factors involved in students' reading development simultaneously.

More recently, Cunningham and Stanovich (1998) reaffirmed the
idea that students' reading development is influenced by the instructional environment:

> Less-skilled readers often find themselves in materials that are
> too difficult for them. . . . The combination of deficient decod-
> ing skills, lack of practice, and difficult materials results in unre-
> warding early reading experiences that lead to less involvement
> in reading-related activities . . . unrewarding reading experiences
> multiply; and practice is avoided or merely tolerated without real
> cognitive involvement. (p. 137)

This excerpt succinctly illustrates the interplay of cognition, affect,
and conation. That is, students' unrewarding reading experiences contribute to negative emotions about reading, which leads to their active

avoidance of reading, and in turn results in fewer opportunities to learn and practice reading strategies.

There are thick threads of affect and conation woven through readers' cognitive operations. Motivation, engagement, self-efficacy, and attributions all influence the acts of reading and the development of our student readers. For example, the self-confident student who faces a challenging reading task will often become motivated to prove herself as a reader. The resulting engagement with text and task includes the use of diverse cognitive strategies and skills. As noted by Allington (1977), "Few can learn to do anything well without the opportunity to engage in whatever is being learned" (p. 60; see also Duke, 2000). It is difficult for students who need to learn to read to do so when they are disengaged from learning.

When we consider the metacognitive, cognitive, affective, conative, and epistemic aspects of reading development, we can envision instruction and classrooms that help students grow and thrive. If reading researchers from the past century, including Moore and Strang, were able to observe contemporary classrooms, they would conclude that at some point in the development of reading instruction a determination was made: to weight heavily students' cognitive strategies and skills development, while giving considerably less attention to developing students' positive affect and empowering conation. Limits to Current faces

The skewed attention given to the cognitive aspects of students' reading development, documented by research across a century, continues to this day. It is reflected in reading curricula, classroom instruction, learning standards, and assessments. Many reading curricula include the comprehensive teaching of sound–symbol correspondences, fluency, vocabulary, and comprehension strategies, but lack detailed approaches to helping student readers develop self-efficacy and motivation or to encouraging helpful attributions. Advocates of the "science of reading" maintain that oral language experience and being able to decode words are the keys to reading success (Hanford, 2018), with little or no consideration of readers' motivation, engagement, or self-efficacy. Students' affective and conative needs are not always a focus of instruction, although attending to them is a hallmark of successful teaching (Dolezal, Welsh, Pressley, & Vincent, 2003).

Paying attention to the factors that shape reading and that operate within each student is critical. This holds for cognitive, affective, conative, and epistemic growth. Just as we tailor reading texts and tasks to students' current levels of achievement and anticipated growth in zones of proximal development (Vygotsky, 1978), we should gauge students' development in self-efficacy, metacognition, motivation, and engagement. However, our work should not be focused on single aspects of reader development—say, working for a week on motivation, then followed by a week that highlights self-efficacy. Effective instruction attends to the range of student needs. Indeed, Betts (1940) observed struggling student readers and concluded that their cognitive efforts were strongly influenced by affect, with unhappy outcomes:

> As the typical pupil becomes increasingly frustrated, he may exhibit tension, movements of the body, hands, and feet, he may frown and squint, and he may exhibit other types of emotional behavior characteristic of a frustrated individual. (p. 741)

Similarly, Strang (1961) noted a range of emotions that influences students' reading:

> (These emotions) interact to further influence a student's reading development: The child's responses may be influenced by his anxiety in a strange situation, by his having to say "I don't know" to many questions, and by the depressing sense of failure as the items become harder. Lapses in attention may lower the child's score. Emotional situations and associations may throw him off the track. If he wants very much to read better immediately, he may feel annoyed at not being given instruction in reading. Other interests and sheer fatigue may also influence his responses unfavorably. (p. 418)

With these observations, Betts and Strang provide classroom examples of the diverse factors that influence both the outcomes of single acts of reading and students' overall reading development. Moreover, there is the accumulation of experience that can steer our students toward or away from reading.

The preceding excerpts, sampled from 100 years of inquiry into reading development, describe researchers' interest in cataloging and characterizing the influences on reader growth, as well as the complex interactions of these factors. The cognitive, affective, and conative factors that operate before, during, and after reading have been widely researched. Each factor has a demonstrated effect on students' reading development and reading achievement. The factors have been addressed—or ignored—in various ways by mainstream reading instruction. Current approaches to reading instruction favor the strategy and skill emphasis on teaching reading over teaching readers, but this emphasis is not for lack of research on affect and conation or an understanding of what student readers need to fully develop.

(CHAPTER REVIEW)

1. Describe the contribution of reading research and reading theory to our understanding of students' reading development and reading achievement.

2. Do you believe that current reading instruction reflects our breadth and depth of knowledge of student' reading development? Why or why not?

3. Explain why classroom instruction should focus on the cognitive, affective, and conative influences on student readers' growth. Give one example from each category.

4. Based on your understanding of the chapter, provide two examples of how a student's failure to learn can have long-lasting, negative consequences.

5. A colleague suggests that most current reading programs are sufficiently good enough to foster all students' reading success. Explain whether you agree or not with this statement, and provide details to support your opinion.

CHAPTER 5

Testing, the "Science of Reading," and the Media

What explains the phenomenon of understanding reading development broadly, but teaching reading narrowly? Cognitive strategies and skills enjoy a privileged status and are considered the most consequential factor in students' reading development. The focus on cognitive strategies and skills is ongoing (Afflerbach et al., 2008; Pearson et al., 2020), and education policy and testing reinforce the widespread belief that strategies and skills are all that matter for students' reading development and achievement, with the result that other aspects of reading growth are not given sufficient attention.

The current hyperfocus on cognition in reading instruction can be traced to several factors. A century ago, Theisen (1920) used test scores to describe students' reading development. He reported:

> The results of standardized tests have everywhere revealed wide differences in (students') reading ability. They have shown decided variations in such factors as rate of reading, knowledge of vocabulary, ability to gather thought from the printed page, and ability to read orally. (p. 560)

This excerpt is important for several reasons. First, it illustrates that our vision of students' reading development and of the important outcomes of our reading instruction is constrained by what we look for. When all you have is a hammer, everything looks like a nail; when all you have is a test, reading looks like strategies and skills. With schools and society focused on tests, the narrative of students' reading development is told with test scores. Lost is the fact that test scores can only tell us about students' growth in relation to what is tested—strategies and skills and the contents of the texts our students read. Second, and correspondingly, test scores are a thin account of what comprises student readers' success or failure. Raw scores, percentile rankings, and stanines provide no specifics about student reader enthusiasm, self-concept, perseverance, or mindfulness. Third, the emphasis on strategies and skills has been persistent from the earliest investigations of reading development: Theisen's 1920 perspective on students' reading ability anticipates the widespread use of test scores to describe students' growth and of the products of students' reading strategies and skills as proxies for development.

TESTING AND THE SELF-FULFILLING PROPHECY

It turns out that test scores are key players in a self-fulfilling prophecy. Consider a test score that indicates a student's underperformance in reading. In our classrooms, we act quickly with this information to identify instruction that addresses the student's indicated need. This is right and good, as long as the test (or quiz or end of week assessment) is valid and reliable. But we will be working on behalf of the student only within the parameters of what is tested: strategies and skills. This fact is often overlooked, because in the 21st century we have become habituated to tests and testing. A well-established testing tradition contributes to society's general failure to ask, "Do tests speak to all the valued outcomes of our good teaching?" Current testing culture shapes curriculum and instruction. In this context, if we want all our students to succeed, we will teach so that our students gain higher test scores. Basing instruction on test scores locks us into the narrow reading strategy and skill perspective. When measures of our students' reading development are tests, our narratives of student success and challenge are told with test scores.

A related issue is that consequential government policy in reading is guided by test scores. Teaching in the schoolhouse is heavily influenced by the agenda of the statehouse. Reading instruction reflects federal, state, and local laws. These laws are informed by documents and initiatives, including the National Reading Panel (NRP) Report (National Institute of Child Health and Human Development, 2000) and the Common Core State Standards (National Governors Association Center for Best Practices & Council of Chief State School Officers, 2010). An examination of both initiatives helps illustrate their obvious and at other times nuanced influence regarding how reading is taught and the learning outcomes expected from "high-quality" instruction.

The NRP Report (2000) identified five cognitive strategy and skill areas to be the focus of teaching reading: phonemic awareness, phonics, fluency, vocabulary, and comprehension. The NRP described these five strategies and skills as:

> instructional topics of widespread interest in the field of reading education that have been articulated in a wide range of theories, research studies, instructional programs, curricula, assessments, and educational policies. *The Panel elected to examine these and subordinate questions because they currently reflect the central issues in reading instruction and reading achievement.* (*www.nichd.nih.gov/publications/ nrp/upload/smallbook_pdf.*, p. 3; italics added)

Consider the claim that the strategies and skills of phonemic awareness, phonics, fluency, vocabulary, and comprehension are " . . . the central issues in reading instruction and reading achievement." From this statement one can infer that students' reading strategies and skills explain the differences between successful and struggling readers. In one sense, this is accurate because the tests used to measure students' reading growth focus exclusively on these cognitive aspects of development. However, our most recent understanding of reading suggests that there are many "central issues" that contribute to students' reading development and achievement. They include metacognition, self-efficacy, motivation and engagement, attributions, and epistemic knowledge. None of these factors were examined in the NRP Report; indeed, they garnered hardly a mention.

The NRP Report, now more than 2 decades old, was based on a review of reading research that met specific criteria for inclusion. And, as we know, this research became the basis for government-certified reading instruction—teaching reading—demanded by Reading First. Here is an account of how research was included in (or left out of) the NRP Report (*www.nichd.nih.gov/publications/nrp/upload/smallbook_pdf*):

> To be included in the (National Reading Panel) database, studies had to measure reading as an outcome. Reading was defined to include several behaviors such as the following: reading real words in isolation or in context, reading pseudowords that can be pronounced but have no meaning, reading text aloud or silently, and comprehending text that is read silently or orally. (p. 5)

From the start, tests had outsized influence on related recommendations for reading instruction. To "measure reading as an outcome," research focused exclusively on cognitive strategies and skills, and the measure was taken by tests of reading subskills (e.g., phonological awareness, phonics, reading single words in isolation, pronunciation of nonsense words). The NRP considered only those research studies that used test scores to determine a statistical significance in differences between treatment and control groups' test scores. The scores reflect measurements of students' cognitive strategies and skills, including phonics, word recognition, oral reading fluency, vocabulary acquisition, and reading comprehension.

Thus, the ideas forwarded by the NRP Report about how our student readers develop were limited by the outcomes that were assessed and how they were assessed. The NRP Report included research that informs *teaching reading*, such as helping students develop the ability to pronounce pseudowords and single words in isolation. Outcomes that inform *teaching readers*, including the establishment and maintenance of students' self-efficacy, increased motivation and engagement related to reading, or the independence gained through metacognitive growth were not included. In part, this outcome was due to a paucity of research that fit the NRP conceptualization of research. Research on reading development that did not include tests of cognitive strategies and skills is not to be found in the report of the NRP. This approach to synthesizing reading research resulted in no attention given to "other" important reading outcomes: "un-included" research involves all aspects of students' reading development that are not strategies and skills. In addition, the commercial reading programs purchased with monies from the U. S. government through the Reading First program were vetted to determine that they focused on the "big 5" reading strategies and skills identified by the NRP. Since the "big 5" was the only standard of inclusion required, predictably, key noncognitive aspects of children's reading development were ignored.

The authors of the NRP Report had concerns about how the report would be interpreted. They noted that aspects of students' reading development that were not included in the report should not be ignored, or assigned secondary importance, in policy, theory, or practice. The Report included the following advice: "The Panel's silence on other topics should not be interpreted as indicating that other topics have no importance or that improvement in those areas would not lead to greater reading achievement" (National Institute of Child Health and Human Development, 2000, p. 3).

This caveat, however, was lost in translation. The U.S. Department of Education made exactly this erroneous interpretation when it used the NRP Report to develop reading education policy and funding; the Report was the salient foundation on which the No Child Left Behind Act and the subsequent Reading First initiative were based. In accordance with these federally funded education initiatives, states applying for Reading First grants were required to purchase reading instruction programs that were based on "scientific evidence" from reading research. Few would argue against reading programs being based on research-proven instructional approaches that address students' reading needs. However, federal law guaranteed that the "scientific evidence" used to evaluate, compare, and label reading programs as "acceptable" would be test scores: measures of students' strategy and skill use.

A result was that elementary reading instruction programs were given the seal of approval from the U. S. Department of Education *only* if they were based on research that found statistically significant differences between experimental treatment and control-group learning outcomes. The dependent variables in this research were reading test scores—a proxy for students' cognitive reading strategies and skills. The use of test scores to deem particular reading instruction programs worthy of Reading First funding mimicked the NRP's use of test scores to determine significant research outcomes and to certify cognitive strategy and skill research as the path to reading achievement. "Acceptable" reading instruction programs focused on the "big 5" (phonemic awareness, phonics, fluency, vocabulary, and comprehension), and student growth in these strategies and skills was measured by tests.

If these circumstances were not enough to limit attention to the important affective, conative, and epistemic aspects of teaching readers, reading tests are also the ongoing and required indicator of schoolwide achievement. The determination that schools exhibit adequate yearly progress (AYP) in grades 3 through 8 is made using test scores that represent students' reading progress exclusively as cognitive strategy and skill development. There are no measures or evaluations related to students' growth in reading affect, metacognition, attributions, self-efficacy, or motivation to read. To reiterate, the use of test scores results in reading programs that are labeled "evidence based." Under this regime, student readers' development in areas other than cognitive strategies and skills is not officially recognized.

Alexander, James, and Glaser (1987) offer a final example of how testing habits and traditions influence classroom practices. When examining the results of the National Assessment of Educational Progress, they observed the following:

> Many of those personal qualities that we hold dear—resilience and courage in the face of stress, a sense of craft in our work, a commitment to justice and caring in our social relationships, a dedication to advancing the public good in communal life—are exceedingly difficult to assess. And so, unfortunately, we are apt to measure what we can, and eventually come to value what is measured over what is left unmeasured. The shift is subtle and occurs gradually. (pp. 51-52)

I propose that current education policy, laws, and school practices too often lead us "to value what is measured over what is left unmeasured," and that these factors contribute to the current situation—in which we know better, but often do not teach better.

Closely aligned with high-stakes reading tests are standards. The CCSS continue the national fixation on reading strategies and skills. The English/Language Arts Common Core State Standards (National Governors Association Center for Best Practices & Council of Chief State School Officers, 2010) describe increasingly complex cognitive outcomes that are expected from students as they matriculate across grades. The affiliated assessment consortia, Smarter Balanced and Partnership for Assessment of Readiness for College and Careers, produce tests with an exclusive focus on cognitive strategies, skills, and content-area knowledge gain that reinforce the idea that the development of student readers' cognitive strategies and skills is all that matters.

Here is how the CCSS, under the heading of "Students Who are College and Career Ready in Reading, Writing, Speaking, Listening, & Language," describe successful students:

- They demonstrate independence.
- They build strong content knowledge.
- They respond to the varying demands of audience, task, purpose, and discipline.
- They comprehend as well as critique.
- They value evidence.
- They use technology and digital media strategically and capably.
- They come to understand other perspectives and cultures.
  (*www.corestandards.org/ELA-Literacy/introduction/students-who-are-college-and-career-ready-in-reading-writing-speaking-listening-language*)

A reading of these CCSS standards may suggest that instruction is moving to a position from which teaching readers is possible, and where attention to motivation and self-efficacy are part and parcel of reading instruction. The CCSS, as well as individual state standards for literacy and reading, describe outcomes of increasing accomplishment and complexity. However, the standards have a clear and exclusive cognitive base, and related educational outcomes remain exclusively cognitive.

The No Child Left Behind Act and the CCSS continue to influence reading instruction, and they share the devotion to cognition and the elimination of almost anything else that matters in teaching readers. In fact, the CCSS are explained as follows to parents: "The new standards also provide a way for teachers to measure student progress throughout the school year and ensure that students are on the pathway to success in their academic careers" (*www.corestandards.org/what-parents-should-know*). The idea that motivation, self-efficacy, or attributions should receive attention in helping students progress toward meeting standards is hardly mentioned or not mentioned at all.

To this point, we've reviewed the histories of reading research, government initiatives and related policies, testing practices, and current standards with the intention of illustrating why the focus on teaching reading and not teaching readers persists. Unfortunately, an additional factor fosters the narrow conceptualization of strategy and skill as paramount in reading—the media. Popular media pose a substantial challenge to the movement *from* teaching reading *to* teaching readers. This challenge emanates from the well-publicized narratives that pose a single factor as the cause of students' reading problems, and then propose a single solution to the problem. In doing so, the popular media misrepresent the complexity of becoming a reader, present questionable accounts of teaching and learning, and veer toward sensationalism.

INFLUENCE OF THE MEDIA

The skewing of resources to the cognitive narrative of how students achieve reading success is aided by the media. The recent focus on the "science of reading" (e.g., Hanford, 2018) perpetuates the narrow conceptualization of reading as cognition and students' reading development as solely a cognitive phenomenon. The media feed the belief that research on cognition in reading is the only legitimate source for informing reading instruction. Actually, there are many sciences of reading (Dewitz & Graves, 2021; McPhee, Handsfield, & Paugh, 2021), and these sciences are supported by voluminous research and well-articulated theories that matter to reading research, theory, and practice. Consider the following insight from Henk, Marinak, and Melnick:

> Literacy professionals have long believed that affective factors can influence the behavior and achievement of developing readers and writers. Research has borne out these intuitions about attitude, motivation, and self-perception so much so that little doubt remains about whether affect has an impact on literacy learning. (2013, p. 311)

There also is the well-researched science of motivation and reading (Guthrie & Wigfield, 2000; Wigfield & Eccles, 2020). There is the science of self-efficacy and reading (Schunk & Bursuck, 2016; Schunk & DiBenedetto, 2020). There is the science of attributions and reading (Brummelman & Dweck, 2020; Dweck, 1975). There is the science of student readers' epistemic development (Lee, Goldman, Levine, & Magliano, 2016). And so it goes. Referencing all of the sciences of reading contributes to the ongoing evolution of our understanding of how reading works, how it develops, and how to foster students' reading growth. It informs how we teach readers. However, only a narrow sampling of scientific evidence currently informs reading instruction programs.

Measures of the impact of reading research include how research findings fare in the marketplace of ideas and how they influence classroom learning. Research is informed by, and influences, theories of reading. Research should also influence classroom practice, although the research-to-practice path is rarely straightforward. The current paths are shaped by the undue influence the media exert on the popularity (and hence value) of particular ideas about reading and reading development. The media are ostensibly resellers of information—and their selective sampling of research, pseudoresearch, and claims (substantiated and unsubstantiated) creates particular narratives of reading development. This sampling is done always with an eye on viewership and readership; websites, media networks, newspapers, and magazines must have market share to survive (Bourdieu, 1999). Decisions about how to gain and maintain market share may (or may not) include a consideration of the representativeness of information included in articles, stories, videos, or

Internet news clips. My contention here is that the *popularity* of a research result used in media accounts is not necessarily equivalent to *value* of the same research result for positively influencing students' reading development. Particular reading research results may be oversold or undersold. They may be ignored or promoted or misrepresented. It is not difficult to find examples of these phenomena.

Consider the following excerpts from "Hard Words: Why Aren't Kids Being Taught to Read?" (2018), written by Emily Hanford, which appears in APM *Reports*:

1. "The prevailing approaches to reading instruction in American schools are inconsistent with basic things scientists have discovered about how children learn to read."
2. "Many educators don't know the science, and in some cases actively resist it. The resistance is the result of beliefs about reading that have been deeply held in the educational establishment for decades, even though those beliefs have been proven wrong by scientists over and over again."
3. "Most teachers nationwide are not being taught reading science in their teacher preparation programs because many deans and faculty in colleges of education either don't know the science or dismiss it. As a result of their intransigence, millions of kids have been set up to fail."
(*www.apmreports.org/story/2018/09/10/hard-words-why-american-kids-arent-being-taught-to-read*)

Where to start? First, how insulting to the tens of thousands of successful, dedicated teachers and administrators who have helped student readers reach their potential! Second, if we vetted the contents and claims of the Hanford article (represented by these excerpts) using the criteria for judging the validity of reading research and the quality of published manuscripts in respected research journals—a process at the heart of science—the text would be rejected for publication. It contains unsubstantiated claims ("The prevailing approaches to reading instruction in American schools are inconsistent with basic things scientists have discovered about how children learn to read," and "Many educators don't know the science, and in some cases actively resist it."); unproven generalizations ("the prevailing approaches to reading instruction in American schools . . . "); unwarranted generalizations ("Most teachers nationwide are not being taught reading science in their teacher preparation programs because many deans and faculty in colleges of education either don't know the science or dismiss it."); and unsupportable inferences ("As a result of their intransigence, millions of kids have been set up to fail."). The article uses unscientific reasoning to falsely claim a scientific high ground and assigns blame to schools of education, reading programs, and classroom teachers for students' test scores, all the while touting the "science of reading."

It is a bit of a surprise then when Hanford discusses the results of an intensive phonics program in Bethlehem, Pennsylvania, that she offers as evidence of superior approaches to teaching reading: "It's impossible to know if the science of reading training is what led to the test score gains." This statement is contrary to the hypothesis of the article—that adhering to the "science of reading" with related instructional materials and training for teachers *is* responsible for test score gains. In addition, the author notes: "Some of the schools in the district moved from half-day to full-day kindergarten the same year the training began, so that could have been a factor" (*www.apmreports.org/story/2018/09/10/hard-words-why-american-kids-arent-being-taught-to-read*).

In any scientific experiment, control is necessary to prevent, mitigate, or monitor the influence of intervening variables. That Hanford mentions the fact that the school day was essentially doubled for some students and that the extended day "could have been a factor" in students' changed reading outcomes dispels any notion that the article is scientific in its portrayal of the "science of reading." Needless to say, "Hard Words: Why aren't kids being taught to read?" brings welcome attention to the topic of reading education and instruction. But, when claims are not backed by evidence yet are still considered valid, science breaks down.

Consider also a recent Public Broadcasting Service (2019) presentation, "What parents of dyslexic children are teaching schools about literacy," which appeared on the nationally syndicated program *PBS News Hour.* This presentation describes the struggles children encounter as they try to learn to read. Parents and relatives provide emotional—and sometimes wrenching and tearful—descriptions of children's inability to read and the children's related alienation, frustration, and diminished self-esteem. Again, the "science of reading" is invoked to bolster the claim that when students receive intensive phonics instruction, reading problems are solved. In addition, the PBS segment claims that dyslexia affects "1 in 5 individuals," without giving a detailed definition of what dyslexia is or providing evidence that supports the claim that 20% of children in U.S. schools have dyslexia. Rarely is elementary school reading instruction a topic of national news; here, PBS has selected a particular perspective on reading, reading development, and reading struggles to support the idea that teaching reading—in this case intensive phonics—will solve the reading problem. It is a pitch for teaching reading, and not teaching readers.

Viewers of the "What parents of dyslexic children are teaching schools about literacy" segment cannot but be moved by the parents' emotions and dedication to their children. However, the information provided in the PBS broadcast does not indicate that the parents and guardians of the profiled children or the narrators and producers of the show considered alternative explanations for the lack of students' reading progress. The broadcast does not explain how "what parents of dyslexic children are teaching schools about literacy" is the result of a judicious sampling from the reading research base that describes all the factors that influence students' reading struggles. For example, consider the demographics for the state of Arkansas, where the PBS segment was recorded. The state, which PBS claims parents are "teaching schools about literacy," ranks 40th with regard to the quality of the state's education system,[1] 35th in per pupil spending,[2] 43rd in average teacher salary,[3] and 4th in the number of poor children.[4] An examination of research that documents how poverty, education financing, and children's exposure to environmental threats might provide competing explanations for why not all children are learning to read, as would research on metacognition, motivation and engagement, self-efficacy, or students' attributions for reading performance, is completely missing.

PBS is ranked first as the "most trusted public institution" in the United States.[5] That PBS is so trusted, and that it presents such a narrow view of students' reading challenges, purported causes, and a proposed solution is a telling case study of how the media selectively sample

---

[1] www.usnews.com/news/best-states/rankings/education

[2] www.governing.com/gov-data/education-data/state-education-spending-per-pupil-data.html

[3] www.teacherportal.com/teacher-salaries-by-state

[4] www.childrensdefense.org/wp-content/uploads/2020/02/The-State-Of-Americas-Children-2020.pdf

[5] www.pbs.org/about/blogs/news/for-17th-consecutive-year-americans-name-pbs-and-member-stations-as-most-trusted-institution

research. That the media assign value to particular types of reading research, in this case research wrapped in the cloak of the "science of reading," could not be more obvious.

The PBS presentation raises the questions of "what role does research play in influencing school practice?" as well as "how does the media select research for inclusion, and to what end?"—which are always worthwhile questions. If one were to buy into Hanford's narrative or the PBS account of parents teaching schools about literacy, it follows that the only solution to students' reading problems is teaching cognitive strategies and skills. I note that although the "science of reading" movement proposes a solution that is limited to strategies and skills, it presents an even narrower idea of the array of strategies and skills needed to be a successful reader (Pearson et al., 2020). Media presentations like the PBS program are sensational. They veer toward the oppositional and confrontational (e.g., "As a result of their [teachers, deans, and faculty in colleges of education] intransigence, millions of kids have been set up to fail"; Hanford, 2018), instead of cooperative. From these positionings, there is little opportunity afforded for constructive dialogue; wholesale dismissal of bodies of reading research lessens or eliminates the possible impact of research that could inform models of reading and reading development, as well as teaching readers. Further, when students' reading progress (or lack thereof) is pinned to one aspect of reading development (and corresponding reading research), the possibility of considering additional mediating factors in that development is lost. The inaccurate narrative that learning cognitive strategies and skills are all that are needed to create thriving readers is perpetuated.

In summary, much is known about how student readers develop. Across the past century, there have been many contributions to this evolving understanding. Unfortunately, all that we know—all that the research describes—about reading development and achievement does not regularly inform reading curriculum and instruction. Too often, schools teach reading, rather than readers. Teaching readers can be informed by the vast research base about all the factors that influence student growth. However, testing practices, governmental policy, skewed media accounts of effective reading instruction, and an exclusionary "science of reading" support the continued prevalence of strategy and skill instruction and pay no attention to motivation and engagement, metacognition, self-efficacy, attributions, and epistemic knowledge.

(CHAPTER REVIEW)

1. Provide a comprehensive description of the influence of testing on the nature of current reading instruction.

2. Should the research influencing reading instruction be labeled the "science of reading" or the "sciences of reading?" Explain your response.

3. How does the media influence reading instruction?

4. The chapter includes a discussion of television productions related to students' reading, including "What parents of dyslexic children are teaching schools about literacy." What is your reaction to the idea that parents can teach schools about literacy?

5. A television show claims that parents in Arkansas are upset with their children's failure to advance as readers. The blame for this failure is attributed to teachers and the reading instruction program. What are alternative explanations for this failure?

(PART II)

TEACHING READERS

Examining the Factors That Influence
Reading Development and Reading Achievement

It's a healthy idea, now and then, to hang a question mark
on things you have long taken for granted.
—BERTRAND RUSSELL

D iverse and dynamic factors influence our students' reading development. These factors may benefit or detract from a single act of
student reading, and they can influence the entire developmental
trajectory of student reading. In Part II, I examine each factor in depth,
focusing on metacognition, self-efficacy, motivation and engagement,
attributions, and epistemic beliefs, as well as on how each of these
powerful factors may interact as students read. I consider how they
influence student readers and consider approaches to instruction that
promote students' growth and achievement as we teach readers.

Chapter 6 introduces several of the most significant "other" factors
that influence reading development, each of which is then examined,
in turn, in the five chapters that follow. Also described in Chapter
6 are the ways in which these factors interact, creating or reinforcing positive and negative aspects of reading development. Chapters
7 through 11 follow a similar structure. I begin with an overview of
the particular factor—for example, metacognition in Chapter 7—and a
description of the importance of the factor for reading development and
reading achievement. Next, I sample the relevant science, considering
the extensive published research and theory that illustrate the power

of the particular factor in reading. This sampling also serves to illustrate that there are "sciences of reading," and that student growth and
achievement are not tied to a singular notion of a "science of reading."
I then consider the classroom implications for instruction and learning, examining examples of curriculum and instruction that contribute
to successful student readers' growth. This discussion is followed by a
consideration of the means with which students' development can be
evaluated in relation to the factor. Assessment that charts students'
growth in all the diverse factors addressed by teaching readers provides
both formative information that optimizes instruction and summative information that can be used to indicate the wide-ranging and
beneficial effects of teaching readers. I also investigate the interrelationships among these factors, for example, how metacognition influences
self-efficacy or motivation and engagement. Finally, in the Appendix, I
introduce a new tool, the *Healthy Readers Profile,* which offers a starting
point for creating detailed reports of students' reading development in
relation to all of the factors discussed in this book.

Introduction to the "Other" Factors That Matter in Students' Reading Development and Achievement

In contrast to portrayals of a narrow "science of reading" and claims that effective phonics instruction is *the* key to students' reading success, and in contrast with assertions that strategies and skills make the good reader, scientific research describes the influence of many factors on readers' development. Consider the following examples. The effect of our instruction on students' reading achievement is mediated by reading motivation (Guthrie, Wigfield, & You, 2012). Motivation and engagement are powerful: the negative effects of socioeconomic disadvantage can be "pushed back" in schools where students from low-income homes are actively engaged in print-rich classrooms (Cummins, 2015). Students' enhanced reading comprehension and achievement are related to their self-efficacy, or their belief that they can succeed (Solheim, 2011). Metacognition— essential for successful, independent reading but not addressed by the NRP—contributes to reading development and reading achievement. Struggling readers can learn metacognitive strategies (Palincsar & Brown, 1984), and these strategies improve reading comprehension (Silven, 1992; Tregaskes & Daines, 1989). Executive functioning assists readers with managing all aspects of reading tasks, be they simple or complex (Meltzer, 2018). Further, the attributions student readers make for their successes and failures can lead them to consistent effort and success or to disengagement and learned helplessness (Butkowsky & Willows, 1980; Weiner, 1986). Finally, epistemic development contributes to students' reading motivation and achievement (Goldman et al., 2019). By the way, I hope you noticed my choice of research citations in this paragraph, as they help indicate that we've known about the power of these factors to influence student reading for decades.

In addition to the potential power of each factor, the factors frequently interact, creating or reinforcing positive and negative aspects of reading development. For example, when student readers are mindful and metacognitive they engage affective, motivational, and behavioral components that provide them with the capacity to adjust their actions and goals to achieve the desired results (Zeidner, Boekaerts, & Pintrich, 2000). Self-regulated learning, featuring metacognition, involves not only cognitive processes that take place in learning, but also affect, as it helps motivate students to sustain effort and attention in their learning processes (Greene & Azevedo, 2007). High-achieving student readers possess high self-efficacy; they make fewer attributions for their performance to external causes, such as task difficulty, luck, and teacher help (Shell, Colvin, & Bruning, 1995). As readers develop self-efficacy, it is often paired with an increase in motivation (McCrudden, Perkins, & Putney, 2005). Epistemic beliefs influence achievement, as they promote engagement in learning and persistence at challenging tasks (Afflerbach, Cho, & Kim, 2015; Schommer, 1994). Metacognition involves monitoring and evaluating processes that can influence students' epistemic understanding (Richter & Schmid, 2009), and sophisticated epistemic beliefs lead readers to engage in elaborated metacognitive processes (Pieschl, Stallmann, & Bromme, 2014). Thus, the sciences of reading describe diverse independent and interactive factors that impact students' reading development. These are the factors that demand our attention when we are teaching readers. This research and the research examined in Part II support teaching readers in classrooms where motivation and engagement, self-efficacy, metacognition, attributions, and epistemic growth are all acknowledged as contributors to reading development and reading achievement, and where each one is a focus of instruction.

In Part II, I investigate metacognition, motivation and engagement, self-efficacy, attributions, and epistemic beliefs in separate chapters. Prior to the chapter-by-chapter consideration of these significant influences on reading development and achievement, I examine three key concepts for teaching readers in relation to these influences: *Matthew Effects in reading*, *zones of proximal development*, and the *gradual release of responsibility*. We consider how each concept has important implications for teaching readers.

MATTHEW EFFECTS, READING DEVELOPMENT, AND TEACHING READERS

Keith Stanovich was interested in determining why certain elementary school students exhibited early, consistent, and then exponential growth in reading—and equally important—why other students floundered in their early reading experiences, and then fell further and further behind their classmates. Stanovich investigated the relationship between the development of students' reading comprehension and vocabulary. What he found was dubbed "Matthew Effects in reading" (Stanovich, 1986). When Matthew Effects are operating, the "rich get richer," as students' initial success with reading begets ongoing success. A well-developed listening vocabulary combined with decoding provide a rich reading vocabulary, which in turn encourages reading comprehension. In turn, comprehension prowess provides student readers with exposure to an increasing diversity of texts and words, which again aids comprehension. Going forward, students' accumulating experiences, strategies, and knowledge contribute to future reading performance. At the heart of this phenomenon are reciprocal and supporting relationships between different aspects of reading development. Here is a short description of Matthew Effects in reading:

> According to the Matthew Effects theory, literacy skills build upon each other in a snowballing fashion and children who start out with stronger initial foundational reading skills will build their abilities at a faster rate. This underscores the importance of providing young children with high-quality early literacy experiences and offering early identification and intervention services to children who may be at-risk of later reading failure. (Cunningham & Chen, 2014, p. 2)

Although Stanovich focused on the cognitive strategies and skills necessary for reading development, he also positioned Matthew Effects in relation to children's environments. Friends and family, reading materials, and social settings all matter in reading development:

> Children who become better readers have selected (e.g., by choosing friends who read or choosing reading as a leisure activity rather than sports or video games), shaped (e.g., by asking for books as presents when young), and evoked (e.g., the child's parents noticed that looking at books was enjoyed or perhaps just that it kept the

child quiet) an environment that will be conducive to further growth in reading. Children who lag in reading achievement do not construct such an environment. (Stanovich, 1986, p. 382)

Reading research and talented teachers' classroom accomplishments demonstrate that helping students develop strong and positive motivations, increasing their self-efficacy, and fostering an empowering self-awareness contribute to reading achievement. Further, the reciprocity that powers Matthew Effects works for affect and conation. Students' self-efficacy promotes motivation and engagement, and metacognition influences accurate attributions for reading outcomes, similar to the way that Stanovich described the reciprocal contributions of vocabulary and comprehension to reading strategy and skill growth. By invoking the broader environments in which our students turn toward or away from reading, we can consider more supports for, and contributions to, teaching readers. We should be sensitive to students' affective and conative development as well as their use of cognitive strategies and skills.

Matthew Effects also inform our work with struggling readers who suffer from the "poor get poorer" (or "the poor stay poor") syndrome. More than 3 decades ago, Stanovich (1986) noted: "Perhaps just as important as the cognitive consequences of reading failure are the motivational side effects. These are receiving increasing attention from researchers" (p. 389). Our struggling readers are prone to *reverse* Matthew Effects. Their initial reading is not so successful, and instead of building momentum to read more and grow more, there is an increasing hesitancy to read. Reciprocity in this instance contributes to a downward spiral, instead of an upward trajectory. Not all students read voraciously, and not all developing readers experience exponential growth throughout elementary school. Not all students choose reading over attractive alternatives. A student's initial, and then ongoing, lack of success at reading can lead him or her to a cognitive, affective, and conative crossroads, struggling to construct meaning and having little or no inclination to try to read.

Stanovich (1986) notes the stark differences between students who experience early reading success and early reading failure:

> Readers of differing skill soon diverge in the amount of practice they receive at reading and writing activities. They also have different histories of success, failure, and reward in the context of academic tasks. The long-term effects of such differing histories could

act to create other cognitive and behavioral differences between readers of varying skill. . . . There is already some evidence suggesting that differences in self-esteem, rather than being the cause of achievement variability, are actually consequences of ability and achievement. (p. 373)

As the rich get richer, the poor get poorer. Some classmates are accelerating in their reading; struggling readers fall further behind their classmates and fall short of the expected grade-level accomplishments. Struggling readers are often provided additional instruction in reading strategies, as demonstrated by numerous response-to-intervention programs, or additional classroom time devoted to reading. One popular approach communicates to students, "You didn't get it right the first time, so we're going to repeat this until you do." Reteaching and practicing are seen as the keys to student learning.

However, struggling readers' considerable affective and conative needs, including motivation and self-efficacy, may not be addressed. Or the essential needs for metacognition and accurate attributions are overlooked. For these students, a reverse Matthew Effect contributes to the lack of self-efficacy and motivation, poor self-esteem, and errant attributions. Struggling readers' theories of self and attributions for performance may be wildly inaccurate, but they are powerful. When students experience reverse Matthew Effects, we should ask, "Does all the high-quality instruction in the world matter to the student who is convinced that he or she cannot achieve?"

As I write this, I reflect on some of the most difficult-to-reach students I've taught: those who were in my Chapter 1 (the predecessor of Title I) reading classrooms and those who attended summer reading clinics (often reluctantly and most often at their parents' behest), with the goal of improving their reading so as to reduce the gap between them and classmates when they returned to school in the fall. Consider fourth graders who are members of the challenged readers group. Struggling 10- and 11-year-old readers may have spent *one-half of their lives* as members of the "low" reading group, with related "poor" reader experiences. Repeated struggles with reading, poor classroom reading performances, and low standardized test scores send a consistent message to these students that they are not reading well. Their self-efficacy is damaged or missing. Like most human beings, they prefer to avoid activities and situations in which they anticipate failure and the negative feelings that accompany it. These students are motivated instead to avoid reading. The resulting absence of involvement with reading leads to lack of metacognition or monitoring comprehension. And the attributions made by such students may restrict them to the reading rut in which they find themselves.

All of us who teach readers can attest to the reality of Matthew Effects—we have student readers who are unstoppable as well as student readers who struggle to start. The original concept of Matthew Effects in reading focused on the relationship of cognitive aspects—vocabulary and reading comprehension—to reading development. However, cognition is but one of the key drivers of reading success. Students learn many things in our classrooms—some of which are unintended—as part of what they accumulate as they matriculate. We hope that they learn, practice, and use their positive attitude, belief in self, self-awareness, and strategies and skills to become ever-improving readers. But there are other accumulations, including reluctance and avoidance, diminished self-esteem, and lack of effort and attention, that mark struggling readers.

ZONES OF PROXIMAL DEVELOPMENT

Acts of teaching readers can be framed, in part, by zones of proximal development (ZPD; Vygotsky, 1978). Learning involves students progressing from the known to the new. ZPD helps us conceptualize the work space between these two critical points and is defined as:

> the distance between the actual developmental level as determined by independent problem solving and the level of potential development as determined through problem-solving under adult guidance, or in collaboration with more capable peers. (Vygotsky, 1978, p. 86)

Much of contemporary reading instruction—whether teacher developed or presented in a commercial reading program—is based on approaches connected with an idea of the ZPD. Teaching readers involves determining the knowledge and abilities a student possesses and using instruction that builds on that foundation, on what a student can do with assistance, and on what we hope a student can ultimately do independently. Typical approaches to cognitive strategy and skill instruction operate in relation to scope and sequence models—what strategies and skills to teach first, what strategies and skills should follow those already taught and learned, and the specific timing and order of each one.

Implicit in this approach is the "building" of new abilities and knowledge on an already existing foundation.

Proximal is defined as "situated close to" (*www.merriam-webster.com/ dictionary/proximal*). As such, students' proximal development is mentally and temporally close to what a student is doing or what we hope the student is doing. A proximal learning target may reside in the next lesson or in an opportunity that unfolds in an ongoing lesson. The ZPD is a useful frame for teaching readers, in part, because it helps us specify what students know and can do, and what we might next help them achieve. Our understanding of a student's current state of knowledge provides the basis for both future learning and our instruction to foster that learning.

As students learn and practice strategies, they can advance toward skilled reading, which is often marked by automatic and highly fluent cognitive strategies and processing (Afflerbach et al., 2008). As we model, explain, and think aloud about fluency, vocabulary, and comprehension strategies, we may be helping students traverse their ZPD to gain new knowledge. Consider this excerpt of teacher talk, in which think-alouds help students better understand a prediction strategy:

"I am looking at the title of this book: *Exploring Our Neighborhood Park*. Next, I'm asking myself some questions:

- Do I know something about parks?
- What do I know about parks?
- Can I use what I know to make a prediction about the book's contents?
- What it is about?

"I think so! I go to the park in my neighborhood, so that can help me anticipate, or predict, what's going to be in the book. Now I'm looking again at the title of the book as well as the picture on the cover. What does this information tell me? I think the author is giving us a preview of what is inside! My prediction is: We will learn about the things we can do in parks and the people and animals we may see in parks. Now I'll continue reading while I check on the prediction."

Over time, this strategy instruction should result in students' learning and successfully using the targeted strategy. We help students work through the ZPD in using the prediction strategy, with a long-term goal of having students internalize such strategies. Words spoken by the teacher eventually become guides to thinking, imported to students' brains and used independently.

The juxtaposition of ZPD with the teaching of reading strategies is common. This positioning leads to a question: "Are ZPD suitable frames for teaching in relation to our students' motivation and engagement, metacognition, self-efficacy, attributions, and epistemology?" I've given thought to whether or not the ZPD can help achieve our goal of teaching readers and the learning and development that we hope to see in students' lives. Can we model motivation and help students reach new and higher levels of motivation? Can we think aloud about self-efficacy, helping students better understand how it develops, and guide students toward an increased belief in self? Can we demonstrate the development of epistemic knowledge, moving from facts to theories and from either–or choices to "it depends" choices? Can we explain the workings of mindfulness and use curriculum that models and scaffolds metacognition? Can we help students progress from less healthy to more healthy attributions?

The answer to each of these questions, I believe, is a qualified "Yes!" Knowing where our students are in terms of the development of motivation to read, of the metacognitive strength to read independently, and of the self-efficacy to engage in reading is as important as knowing which set of consonant blends and comprehension strategies are best taught next. Consider the following scenario, in which a teacher models self-efficacy for her students:

> "I am looking at the title of this book: *Animals of the Serengeti*. Right before I read a book with new information, I try to think about how well I've read other books:
>
> - I think about that book on dinosaurs—I knew hardly anything about them.
> - But I remembered that I learned a lot from that book.
> - I got to draw some of the dinosaurs I learned about, and our group did the class presentation on carnivores.
> - I remember that I've learned lots of new things from reading books like this.
> - I am thinking of all the times I've encountered new things in a book and then managed to learn that information.
>
> "So, I'm convincing myself that I will do well and that helps me try my hardest. I know I can read and understand, and I'm looking

forward to reading this book. I know I might run into a problem or two in trying to understand this book, but I am ready to give it my all!"

This example of teacher modeling presents students with a self-efficacy perspective—how a reading task can be framed by how we think about ourselves as readers and how past positive reading experiences can be strong reference points. In essence, we are aiming to surround our students with models, explanations, descriptions, and illustrations that give them the means to conceptualize motivation and engagement, self-efficacy, and metacognition; understand their value; and develop increasing facility with these powerful influences on reading development. The ZPD that is commonly used in conjunction with reading strategies and skills can help guide our instruction as we teach readers. We want to make the invisible visible. A challenge is to link the newly visible think-alouds, explanations, and demonstrations to the gradual release of responsibility, with which students assume mindsets that help them develop motivation and engagement, self-efficacy, attributions, and epistemic beliefs, along with the attendant responsibilities.

GRADUAL RELEASE OF RESPONSIBILITY

Teaching reading within the ZPD often invokes teacher scaffolding of strategies and the gradual release of responsibility to students, which involves introducing, maintaining, and then withdrawing support for students as they increasingly take responsibility for using the strategies. The gradual release of responsibility represents the process with which teachers model, explain, and think aloud about aspects of reading and then incrementally withdraw these supports (Pearson, McVee, & Shanahan, 2019). Teaching within ZPD typically follows a pattern such as the following:

- The approach to scaffolding involves a gradual release of responsibility by the teacher and the related gradual acceptance of responsibility by the student. This can be conceptualized as I do (teacher), we do (teacher and student) and ultimately, you do (student).
- The transition from I, to we, to you is discussed and explained.
- The teacher models and explains what is to be learned: a strategy, an attitude, a mindset.

- While providing a full scaffold, the teacher looks for student successes and misunderstandings. Scaffolding is withdrawn or maintained on the basis of observations of students' performance, attitude, and mindset and of some indication that a student is prepared.
- When needed, the teacher can revisit explanations, modeling, and thinking aloud to provide a consistent model for the student to follow and emulate.
- Support is gradually withdrawn, while maintaining scrutiny of student levels of understanding, independence, and success.

Throughout the process, we provide assistance, encouragement, and feedback for students. With time and effort, our hope is that these supports can be reduced as students internalize what were originally an external voice and teacher guidance. Teachers maintain classroom talk that is reflective, supportive, and explanatory, providing a model for remembering, using, and appreciating the different facets of reading development and performance.

It's an ongoing model of reflection, thoughtfulness, making an effort, recognizing challenges, observing how reading contributes to our lives, and celebrating successes. Here is a teacher thinking aloud, with the goal of providing an external model of how motivation and engagement work and influence her reading:

- "I know how much fun reading can be."
- "I can learn more about the things I'm really interested in."
- "I know I can discuss what I'm learning with my classmates."
- "My parents are always happy when I tell them what I've learned from my classes in school."

Teaching, suggesting, reminding, and insinuating that we can and should be motivated to read is important. Students learn from such models, and as they internalize the speech and ideas that we present to them, less and less teacher input is needed. The gradual release of responsibility on our part is complemented by students' gradual acceptance of responsibility, and their growth in incorporating motivation, self-efficacy, and the range of influences on reading. The gradual release of responsibility is also enhanced as we offer reading contexts in which students can experience and "practice" different motivations for reading. Attributions provide models and verbalizations of how effort relates to reading performance and outcome. In modeling self-efficacy, we provide students with examples of how we construct positive self-images as readers and how we connect those images to evidence from our histories as readers. ZPD help us visualize where our students can progress in their motivation, self-efficacy, attributions, and epistemic growth. The gradual release of responsibility provides a means of developing supportive classroom contexts, activities, and discussions that help us support student growth as we teach readers.

(CHAPTER REVIEW)

1. Choose three readers' characteristics from the following list: strategies and skills, motivation and engagement, metacognition, self-efficacy, attributions, and epistemic knowledge. Next, describe how the three characteristics may interact to encourage or stifle student reading development.

2. Describe Matthew Effects and how they benefit developing readers.

3. Describe a negative Matthew Effect and how it presents an obstacle to students' reading development.

4. Explain the nature of successful teaching using the zone of proximal development as a framework.

5. Describe the gradual release of responsibility, and determine if it is a suitable approach for furthering the development of students' motivation and engagement or self-efficacy.

CHAPTER 7

Metacognition, Executive Functioning, and Mindfulness

The aim of good teachers should, of course, be to make themselves redundant. If we are to properly educate others, we must enable them to become independent learners.
—DAVID WHITEBREAD

Successful classrooms are a hive of activity, with students working purposively and independently. When we teach readers, we help them develop independence. Essential to this development is students' awareness—of themselves, of their work, of their resources, of the challenges they may face as they read, and of the progress they make. This chapter focuses on how readers plan, monitor, and control their reading and become mindful and reflective. It discusses how we can help our students develop these abilities. The path to reading independence is rooted in a self-awareness that helps students approach and engage with reading. It involves readers' moment-by-moment work in the midst of reading, as well as understanding why we read, the benefits of reading, and one's self as a reader. When self-awareness is a focus of teaching readers, we can encourage students to become mindful, reflective, and self-sustaining.

I choose metacognition as the topic of the lead chapter in Part II because mindfulness—central to reading success—also represents students' developing an awareness of themselves and their reading. Knowing one's self as a reader involves more than determining how, when, and where to use strategies and if those strategies work. Knowing one's self allows students to understand and appreciate reading's connection to the lives they lead. It follows that metacognition and mindfulness can also contribute to student growth related to building self-efficacy, creating motivation and engagement, and making accurate attributions for reading performance.

There is great variety in the vocabulary used to describe students knowing themselves, knowing learning, and knowing reading. Veenman, van Hout-Wolters, and Afflerbach (2006) noted the diversity of terms used in theory, research, and practice related to metacognitive knowledge:

> Metacognitive beliefs, metacognitive awareness, metacognitive experiences, metacognitive knowledge, feeling of knowing, judgment of learning, theory of mind, meta memory, metacognitive skills, executive skills, higher-order skills, metacomponents, comprehension monitoring, learning strategies, heuristic strategies, and self-regulation are several of the terms we commonly associate with metacognition. (p. 4)

In this chapter I focus on the role of metacognition, executive functioning, and mindfulness in reading. Metacognition reflects student readers' awareness of strategies and skills, and how, when, and why to use them. Metacognition helps students in goal setting, monitoring the construction of meaning, looking out for problems and fixing them, and completing reading tasks in relation to goals. A related phenomenon is executive functioning, which oversees metacognition and helps our student readers manage the tasks of constructing meaning and monitoring that process. Executive functioning helps readers establish and maintain the necessary focus to undertake tasks of varying difficulty. It also operates to distribute memory resources and to help student readers attend to and concentrate on the reading work at hand. Metacognition and executive functioning are important factors in teaching readers that are encapsulated by a third important factor, mindfulness. Mindfulness is reflected in our students' awareness of their thoughts, actions, strategies, feelings, and emotions. Mindful student readers are in the moment. Mindfulness is a glue that binds together cognition, affect, and conation during reading. It helps student readers understand and appreciate their motivation and engagement, self-efficacy, attributions, and strategies—and how they work and interact in reading. Even when they are not reading, mindful students understand reading's value and place in their lives. Mindful students are able to reflect on the past and anticipate their future as readers.

Prior to the in-depth consideration of metacognition, executive functioning, and mindfulness, I want to make a comment about working memory. Student readers' accomplishments relate to how well they manage their reading. All readers (all human beings, really) are born with a limited amount of working memory (Baddeley & Hitch, 1974; Jung, 2018; Peng et al., 2018). Working memory is the place where we conduct our reading processes—recognizing words, calling up relevant background knowledge, using comprehension strategies, monitoring progress, critiquing a text or author, managing emotions, maintaining motivation, and building self-efficacy. This is a large amount of brain work—comprising information and processing—for even accomplished readers to manage. Although our brains normally work well within the limitations of working memory, we are reminded of its limits when we attempt two complex tasks at the same time or even try to memorize a number with many digits. The limitations of working memory show themselves when our student readers are "in the weeds," decoding words, searching their prior knowledge for information related to the text, applying strategies, identifying and dealing with challenges to understanding, remembering the goal of reading, and completing complex reading-related tasks. If you recall your attempt to understand the *broadpoint* paragraph in Chapter 2, you may be reminded of how your working memory was challenged by the difficult and unfamiliar text. Trying to construct meaning, reread, identify key vocabulary, parse sentences, and remember what has already been read all tax the memory system. Thus, our work related to metacognition has a goal of helping students manage their limited working memory systems while achieving reading success with varied texts and for varying purposes.

METACOGNITION

Accomplished readers are metacognitive. Experienced learners are metacognitive beings, but the efficiency of our reading can hide the workings of metacognition. A smoothly functioning metacognitive system often operates effortlessly, coordinating and guiding our work until a problem arises or a question emerges (Afflerbach et al., 2008). Metacognition operates behind the scenes—helping us set goals, plan, call up relevant prior knowledge, choose and use strategies, regulate our work, and coordinate the entire suite of these actions. When we are successful, metacognition hardly calls attention to itself, and we may not be aware of it.

Difficult tasks may help us better understand and appreciate our own metacognition—again, reflect on your reading of the challenging *broad-point* paragraph, and you will be reminded of the nature and value of metacognition.

We are not wanting for comprehensive descriptions of the nature and benefits of metacognition or for understanding the implications for teaching readers: Note that the research cited in this chapter ranges over more than 4 decades. I use this array of research evidence not only to demonstrate our accumulated knowledge on metacognition, but also to illustrate that we've known the benefits of metacognition for more than 40 years, and that we have known about the power of reflection and mindfulness for millennia (de Landazuri, 2015). Flavell (1976) is considered a founder of the concept of metacognition, which he described as "one's knowledge concerning one's own cognitive processes or anything related to them" (p. 232). Stewart and Landine (1995) add that metacognition "focuses on the active participation of the individual in his or her thinking process" (p. 17), and Borkowski and Turner (1990) observe that metacognition is "knowledge about cognition, awareness of one's own thinking processes, comprehension of requirements for learning, control of learning processes, and regulation of cognitive procedures" (p. 161). As such, metacognition includes student readers' knowledge of the mental processes and strategies involved in learning and of the strategies that help them control and adjust their learning. Metacognition makes learning more efficient and long lasting. It allows our students to conceptualize, control, and manage learning processes and strategies, contributing to "the mindful regulation of one's own learning processes" (Schneider, 2008, p. 115). Indeed, it is difficult to imagine student learning and independence without metacognition.

Millis (2016) describes metacognition as the key to successful learning, and given the centrality of metacognition to learning and remembering, there is a long-standing interest in understanding how metacognition develops in children. This development can serve as a foundation for students' progress toward independence in reading and in all school subjects. Deanna Kuhn (2000) noted:

> Young children's dawning awareness of mental functions lies at one end of a developmental progression. . . . During its extended developmental course, metacognition becomes more explicit, powerful, and effective, as it comes to operate increasingly under the individual's control. (p. 178)

A focus on metacognition when we are teaching readers can foster this development. Research demonstrates that the path to becoming effectively metacognitive varies by individual student; however, not all children develop to the point where they can independently manage their work. Veenman and colleagues (2006) note that:

> The vast majority of students spontaneously pick up metacognitive knowledge and skills to a certain extent from their parents, their peers, and especially their teachers. . . . Still, a substantial group cannot spontaneously acquire a metacognitive repertoire, either because the opportunity to do so is missing or they do not see the relevance of investing effort in building up such a repertoire. (p. 9)

Our classroom observations and discussions with students affirm this reality: metacognition often distinguishes successful readers from struggling readers. Whether working to decode words and string them together to comprehend a sentence or reading multimedia texts to critically evaluate different authors' perspectives, metacognition must be operating to bring students to the successful completion of reading and related tasks.

Sampling the Science

Research documents how metacognition develops and the central role it plays in reading success. Research also tells us why becoming metacognitive is not a given for all developing readers. For example, Markman (1977) asked elementary school students to read instructions and report on how clearly the instructions were written. She then examined how well students followed the instructions, which included vague text and sections that omitted information. Younger students did not detect many of the obvious omissions or unclear sections in the instructions, and they did not score well on a measure of ability to follow the instructions. Similarly, Flavell, Friedrichs, and Hoyt (1970) asked younger students in kindergarten—and older students in grades 2 and 4—to study in preparation for being asked to recall information. Both older and younger students reported they were ready to recall information after studying. The difference in results was due to the fact that the older students were correct: they accurately judged the amount of studying that was needed to achieve perfect recall. Younger students reported that they too were ready—but their recall was far from perfect. In her investigation of beginning readers' metacognition, Baker (1985) determined that some students did not monitor their comprehension and created inaccurate interpretations of text because they failed to reread and detect and fix emerging comprehension problems. Metacognition serves to trigger fix-it strategies, but without an awareness of difficulties—also provided by metacognition—students forego the opportunity to address them.

Garner and Kraus (1981-1982) and Garner and Reis (1981) investigated students with different levels of reading achievement and found that poor readers were not aware that they didn't understand text; this lack of metacognitive awareness denied readers the opportunity to attempt to fix their misunderstandings and resulted in lower comprehension. Myers and Paris (1978) compared sixth-grade good and poor readers and found that the less able readers had limited knowledge of comprehension-monitoring strategies. The less able readers considered reading to be a process of decoding, as opposed to a process of comprehending, and it was not surprising that the less able readers used fewer metacognitive, comprehension-monitoring strategies. Based on the findings of all these studies, the array of metacognitive strategies and mindsets that benefit developing readers has become increasingly clear. They include setting realistic goals, monitoring comprehension, rereading, detecting problems, and fixing them. Metacognition involves reading with the goal of making meaning and monitoring progress at constructing this meaning. Sampling the science—including research and related theory building—affirms as well that metacognition is essential for students' reading success.

Fostering our developing readers' metacognitive ability should be a priority. For reading, literacy, and all school endeavors, it is important to determine where our students are positioned in the arc of development toward "powerful" and "effective" metacognition and how our instruction can complement this growth. Whitebread and colleagues (2009) determined that the onset of metacognition can occur as early as years 3 through 5, and that it often occurs when children are involved in self-initiated learning, working in small groups, and collaborating and talking with peers. From these beginnings, metacognition normally develops to become "more sophisticated and academically oriented whenever formal education requires the explicit utilization of a metacognitive repertoire" (Veenman et al., 2006, p. 8). As students further mature, metacognition influences both intrinsic motivation and reading comprehension (Miyamoto, Pfost, & Artelt, 2019).

Student readers' ongoing metacognitive development, built on a stable and early foundation, is central to their success with increasingly complex texts and related tasks. Recent intervention studies examined the influence of metacognition instruction on young children's comprehension. Jiang and Davis (2017) taught comprehension-monitoring strategies to kindergarten and PreK students as they listened to stories, and determined that these students performed better than schoolmates who didn't receive this metacognitive strategy instruction. A conclusion was that young children's listening comprehension could serve as the initial "place" for learning and practicing metacognition and as a base for using metacognition in nascent reading comprehension. Schneider (2008) found that "even children 7–8 years of age can be taught to monitor the relative efficacy of strategies that they are using and to use utility information gained from monitoring in making future strategy selections" (p. 119). Boulware-Gooden, Carreker, Thornhill, and Joshi (2007) demonstrated that learning metacognitive strategies increased third-grade students' reading comprehension and vocabulary achievement. Likewise, third graders trained in a program designed specifically to foster metacognition (Connor et al., 2018) demonstrated superior reading comprehension performance.

Palincsar and Brown (1984) created instruction to help struggling middle school readers develop metacognitive reading routines. Their work was based, in part, on the examination of expert readers' use of metacognition: "When a comprehension failure is detected, readers must slow down and allot extra processing to the problem area. They must employ debugging devices or active strategies that take time and effort" (p. 118). Reciprocal teaching helped these students add metacognitive mindsets and strategies to their reading toolkit. Further, the middle school students learned to monitor comprehension by previewing text and then setting personal comprehension checkpoints throughout the text; students' metacognitive learning was scaffolded using worksheets (Fogarty et al., 2017).

In summary, research on metacognition, conducted across the last 4 decades, demonstrates that it is a necessary and powerful component of students' reading, and that helping students develop metacognitive mindsets and strategies should be emphasized in teaching readers. There is a rich research base that examines the nature of metacognition and how it develops. This research details students' strategies and mindsets and the common challenges to developing students' metacognitive reading routines. Related research documents the metacognitive needs of student readers and how instruction can meet those needs as they develop mindfulness and self-awareness.

Although research describes metacognition as a "must have" for successful reading, it may not be a regular focus of reading programs and teaching materials. The promise of metacognition is not consistently realized in classroom instruction. As students are learning phonemic awareness, phonics, fluency, vocabulary, and comprehension, they should be developing the means to use, coordinate, and evaluate these reading strategies and skills on their own. Lacking metacognition, our students do not understand (and appreciate) how the different aspects of reading work together: knowing that effort can contribute to success or knowing that past reading successes motivate us to pursue future reading. Just as we are vigilant with younger students who are struggling to learn the mechanics of reading, we also should be vigilant with our students who are not developing metacognitive awareness.

We can teach readers so that they develop metacognition that helps them attain both immediate and more distant reading goals. The former goal relates to monitoring the construction of meaning while reading words, phrases, and sentences. For example, consider the student who encounters key but unfamiliar words, such as *peak* or *revolution*. Prompted by metacognition, the student (1) realizes that the word is unfamiliar and the meaning is not known, (2) flags the word as a challenge to be dealt with, (3) works to unlock the meaning of the unfamiliar word, (4) determines the degree of success with the unfamiliar word, and (5) resumes reading to construct meaning. The power of metacognition is most often portrayed in relation to such comprehension monitoring and evaluation of ongoing work—the work that readers do to set goals, check on progress toward meeting goals, detect problems, and fix them. The same reader who uses metacognition to help uncover the meaning of *peak* is also gauging progress toward reading goals, which may include understanding a paragraph and determining if those reading goals have been met.

In addition to this "in the moment" support of reading provided by metacognition, a second set of metacognitive benefits accrues. Student readers who are self-aware make connections between different aspects of their reading: their efforts, their accomplishments, and what they learn from reading and their growth in reading. For example, metacognition helps developing readers better understand how engagement influences their reading performance. Further, an awareness of giving effort and understanding how it contributes to reading success build self-efficacy and enable students to make mentally healthy attributions for the outcomes of their performance. It is here that metacognition interfaces with affect and conation. As students acquire self-awareness, they better understand how motivations and attitudes influence their reading performance. They better understand how their prior knowledge and experience contribute to reading success and how lack of such knowledge makes reading more difficult. They understand how their degree of effort contributes to successful reading. They are aware of the source of their pride for a reading job done well.

EXECUTIVE FUNCTIONING AND SELF-REGULATED LEARNING

The metacognition detailed in the prior section helps students conduct a fine-grained analysis of their reading as it happens and both manage and evaluate their work. As we teach readers, we want also to focus on executive functioning and self-regulation, which further helps student readers coordinate and improve their reading. According to the Center on the Developing Child:

> Executive function helps readers as they are following complex instructions, planning and working towards different goals, attending to construction of meaning and related reading tasks, focusing on the work at hand even when there are distractions to this work, and practicing self-control.
> (*https://developingchild.harvard.edu/resources/what-is-executive-function-and-how-does-it-relate-to-child-development*)

Schneider (2008) describes the close connection between metacognition (or "self-monitoring") and executive functioning:

> Self-monitoring and self-regulation correspond to two different levels of metacognitive processing that interact very closely. Self-monitoring refers to keeping track of where you are with your goal of understanding and remembering (a bottom-up process). In comparison, self-regulation or control refers to central executive activities and includes planning, directing, and evaluating your behavior (a top-down process). (p. 117)

Self-regulation involves the strategies used by students to initiate and maintain diverse behaviors and to manage cognition and affect with the intention of reaching a goal. These goals vary—they may focus on comprehending a difficult paragraph, reading deeply to conduct a critique of the author's style, or using what is understood from a text to solve a challenging problem. Students' self-regulation can involve developing a plan for reading, paying attention and concentrating, managing resources and time, and learning and remembering important information. Levels of executive control and children's self-regulation are closely related to their reading comprehension (Raudszus, Segers, & Verhoeven, 2018).

Executive functioning and self-regulation are the master of ceremonies—managing the processes, strategies, reflections, emotions, and feelings that are involved in the acts of reading. Consider your students as they attempt to meet a Common Core State Standard, read and synthesize several texts for a report, or work to meet another similarly complex challenge. Students must read, remember, check on their progress, and anticipate using what they have learned from previous reading in a related task. There is much to manage; executive functioning helps students do so. As managers, executive functioning and mindfulness help control students' goal directedness and help students apply fix-it strategies when needed (while staying focused on the larger reading task), focusing attention when affect may threaten to distract and providing perseverance when facing daunting reading challenges. Self-regulation involves not only the cognitive processes involved in learning, but also the sustaining power of affect, such as the influence of positive motivation, that is needed as students undertake learning challenges (Pintrich, 2002).

To appreciate the importance of executive functioning and self-regulation, we might reflect on a recent or ongoing personal undertaking that demanded of us not only cognitive performance, but coordination of knowledge and emotions as well. These personal examples remind us of how our thinking, or cognition, is not removed from the contexts of emotion, feeling, and personal accomplishment. Our reflections might remind us of a dedicated preparation for taking a graduate program admissions test, writing an autobiography, painting a house or apartment, raising children, diagnosing an engine problem by taking it apart, creating a work of art, or understanding and signing a complex contract. Each of these pursuits is demanding of time and effort and involves thinking and emotion. These interrelated factors must be managed, kept track of, and monitored to make sure they are working in pursuit of the specific goal.

There is an ongoing debate as to when young children might benefit from executive function instruction. Although executive functioning is both complex and demanding, it is not necessary to defer instruction until students have demonstrated learning and mastery in the related cognitive strategies and skills of reading. For example, researchers at the Center on the Developing Child note:

> Contrary to the theory that guides some early education programs that focus solely on teaching letters and numbers, explicit efforts to foster executive functioning have positive influences on instilling early literacy and numeracy skills.
> (*https://developingchild.harvard.edu/resources/what-is-executive-function-and-how-does-it-relate-to-child-development*)

This viewpoint is important for at least two reasons. First, it suggests that we can encourage students' executive functioning and metacognition early in their reading careers. Second, it reminds us that effective reading programs that help us teach readers should focus not only on strategy and skill instruction, but also on self-awareness and metacognition.

MINDFULNESS

Successful readers are mindful—they have the presence of mind to observe, make connections, learn, and act on what they learn from reflection. Although there are various terms that relate to mindfulness, including self-awareness, reflection, metacognition, and executive functioning, I believe "mindfulness" is the most inclusive of these terms. As such, it has the broadest application and relates to cognitive, affective, and conative aspects of teaching readers. *Mindfulness* can be defined as an "awareness of one's thoughts, emotions, or experiences on a moment-to-moment basis" (*www.merriam-webster.com/dictionary/mindfulness*). Mindfulness allows students to connect their successful use of metacognition to positive reading outcomes. It also helps students make the connection between their performance and effort and success. For example, understanding the relationship between their performance, their effort, and a positive outcome cannot help but boost students' self-efficacy. Over time, mindfulness also helps students to reflect on the fact that they were successful, which can boost motivation to read further. Varga (2017) notes that student mindfulness expands from having metacognitive control over strategies and skills to understanding and appreciating reading itself. Students can tap into the related motivational and affective factors that support their reading and reading development. This mindfulness is also reflected in the development of students' critical consciousness, with which students "believe in their own efficacy and the power of schooling to change their lives" (Mehan, Hubbard, & Villanueva, 1994, p. 97). Certainly, helping our students form such beliefs is a goal we can all embrace.

Mindfulness is greater than the sum of metacognition and executive control. According to de Landazuri (2015), mindfulness has been appreciated as far back as Plato, who valued it as "an awareness of the real value of one's own actions" (p. 125). From centuries ago to the here and now of our classrooms, mindfulness involves how readers view themselves, how they go about reading, and how they understand the benefits of reading. Mindful students read with agency and with an awareness of their privileges and responsibilities as readers. In their mindfulness, they understand the nuts and bolts of reading, the purposes for reading, and their roles as readers.

Consider the students who are mindful readers. In addition to monitoring comprehension in relation to an overall reading goal, these readers keep track of the effort put into reading and the rewards for this effort. Mindful readers connect their reading effort with their reading outcomes. In doing so, student readers can create accurate attributions for performance. These readers are also developing self-efficacy because the series of successful reading experiences teaches them that they are capable. Self-knowledge of the history of success combined with an understanding of what makes for successful reading lead students to look forward to future acts of reading. This perception then leads to the desire to return to reading whenever possible because it gives students feelings of accomplishment, pride, and joy. An awareness of what is "gotten" from reading grows, and the reflective students further appreciate how reading contributes to attaining goals. A lesson here is that what comprehension monitoring does for successful cognition, self-awareness does for successful reading and successful readers. Helping students become mindful readers must accompany all our other instructional goals.

TEACHING READERS: METACOGNITION IN THE CLASSROOM

What are the characteristics of effective metacognition instruction? How should we develop and deliver this instruction? Veenman (2015) and Veenman et al. (2006) suggest three general goals in teaching readers:

* use explicit teaching that focuses on the value of metacognition,
* situate metacognition instruction in authentic learning contexts,
* provide continual teaching of metacognitive mindsets and strategies.

First, our instruction should help students understand the value of metacognition in general and in relation to specific classroom reading situations. Teaching metacognition should include explanations of the benefits of metacognition to students. This instruction is especially valuable as students attempt to conceptualize metacognitive thinking and metacognitive strategies, phenomena that are largely invisible. Our good instruction names the metacognitive strategies and mindsets: "Rereading is a great way to make sure you understand this story," and "As we work through this chapter, let's all remember that we are here to make meaning from the text. We should always be asking, Does that make sense?" Our instruction provides preliminary goals for students and offers encouragement for those students who may be overwhelmed by the dual tasks of constructing meaning and establishing metacognitive awareness: "Let's read this long paragraph together, checking at the end of each sentence to make sure that we understand," and "Remember that it's sometimes smart to slow our reading down so that we can take in all that information." Taking on the task of attending to the metacognitive "part" of reading can be daunting for those students who are challenged by the cognitive (i.e., learning and using strategies and skills) part of reading. Therefore, our instruction should be based on an understanding of the metacognitive and cognitive loads created by each reading text and task.

The second feature of effective instruction is the interweaving of metacognition with authentic classroom learning tasks. This approach assumes that students see value in what is being learned in the classroom and invest in that learning; it follows that metacognitive knowledge is used to help guide the learning at hand. When metacognition and the reading curriculum are intertwined, opportunities are provided for students to experience the immediate value of being metacognitive as well as gain the experience of working to achieve two distinct but closely related goals: being metacognitive and learning course content. The value of embedding metacognitive instruction in ongoing classroom learning contexts is also endorsed by Schneider (2008) in his description of effective metacognitive strategy instruction:

Strategy instruction was not carried out in isolation but integrated in the curriculum and taught as part of language arts, mathematics, science, and social studies . . . effective teachers did not emphasize the use of single strategies but taught the flexible use of a range of procedures that corresponded to subject matter, time constraints, and other task demands. (p. 119)

The third principle of effective metacognition instruction is ongoing training that successively builds on preliminary and simple metacognitive routines. For example, beginning readers who learn to ask themselves seemingly simple metacognitive questions like, "Does that make sense?" can benefit from subsequent instruction that helps them ask, "If it doesn't make sense, what is the problem?" and "How can I fix the problem?" In addition, the linking of metacognitive thinking and strategies across grade levels and content areas should be encouraged. Having our students ask, "What is my goal?" and "Am I making progress toward that goal?" are valuable questions to ask for any and all classroom learning in social studies, science, and math. As student readers regularly ask such questions, they become second nature for them, preparing them for increasingly complex texts and tasks as they advance through school. Finally, recall that the students who struggle with metacognition because their working memory is already fully engaged will need time to learn, practice, and master metacognitive routines. An ongoing program of metacognition instruction—across reading development stages, grade levels, and content areas—provides the opportunities for this learning and practice as we teach readers.

Earlier in this chapter, I cited Deanna Kuhn's work that focuses on children's metacognitive development. I want to return to her ideas as we think about teaching students who face increasingly complex reading texts and tasks as they advance through the grades. Kuhn (2000) describes the developmental nature of metacognition and its potential to become a powerful and positive force as it operates under our students' conscious control. In this section, I take Kuhn's idea of metacognitive development and combine it with Veenman and colleagues' (2006) guidelines for metacognition instruction. Then I examine three reading scenarios that illustrate how teaching readers metacognition can anticipate the increasing complexity of students' reading. I examine the metacognitive demand that each task places on student readers and how we can help address these increasing demands.

Picture second-grade students who struggle to "put it all together" in terms of reading and understanding. The students don't have the big picture view of reading: they may not understand how we read, the benefits of reading, the means to manage an act of reading, or why they would want to be readers. For these students, reading is most often a mix of stress and unsuccessful attempts to be strategic. In small groups, Ms. Gutierrez, their teacher, helps the readers set two immediate goals: to be clear about why they are reading and about how to manage their reading. She provides instruction on the mechanics of reading that the students have yet to master: phonics and sound–symbol correspondences in English, building sight-word vocabularies, and linking students' listening comprehension to nascent reading comprehension. Ms. Gutierrez focuses on developing metacognition. She also reads stories and takes note of her students' listening comprehension, regularly asking them about their understanding of text. She engages them in setting goals for reading (or listening to) a story. A primary goal of her instruction—of teaching readers—is to help students begin their careers as metacognitive readers.

Ms. Gutierrez understands the value of metacognition, but also the challenge that it places on students above and beyond the challenge posed by the normal strategies and skills of reading. Accordingly, she starts with a simple story consisting of familiar and phonetically regular words. This instructional approach will help her students manage the limited "bandwidth"—the constraints of working memory—as they work on cognitive and metacognitive tasks. Stories that encourage and reward meaning making not only complement the learning of reading mechanics, but also serve as the metacognitive beacon for the students—who are encouraged to regularly ask themselves, "Does that make sense?" The students then read short stories that have a predictable structure and accessible language, while working with a metacognitive checklist. This checklist helps them do the work of reading and metacognition in the limited space of working memory. It prompts and promotes their emergent metacognition and contains questions that are modeled and discussed prior to using scaffolds and transferring responsibility. The following checklist includes questions for developing readers that I've used in two university reading clinic settings and in teaching elementary grades reading that primarily focuses on meaning making. The questions can be asked at the end of sentences or paragraphs or at key points in stories:

☐ Does that make sense?

☐ Do I understand the story?

As students learn to regularly ask these questions, additional questions that focus on recognizing and dealing with blockages to meaning can be added, as Ms. Gutierrez sees fit:

☐ Is there a problem with my understanding?

☐ What is the problem?

☐ Can I fix it?

☐ How can I fix it?

☐ Did I fix it?

☐ Can I get back on track?

These checklists are intended to help the students focus on reading to comprehend the content and to remind them that asking if a sentence makes sense is good practice. The first question serves as a prompt to the students that we read for meaning. The following questions prompt them to consider particular ways of metacognitive thinking and action. I note that the checklists require students to work hard; the payoff is that they can begin to feel in control of the act of reading—a big step in establishing agency in reading. They can also begin to make connections to how their effort is contributing to reading performance and how a previously insurmountable obstacle was confronted and overcome.

The metacognitive checklists we've just considered can be modified to meet students' individual needs and developmental trajectories. We may have students for whom the seemingly simple question "Does that make sense?" is challenge enough. For those students, an initial focus on this one question may be sufficient. One of our goals with such questions—which we can provide in checklist form—is that students eventually import such questions and checklists into their heads and into their ways of thinking and reading. When students approach reading with the questions (or some variation of these questions) that I've developed in mind, there is a strong base on which to construct more elaborate questions and metacognitive routines.

The habit of asking questions of one's self can then serve as the metacognitive foundation. As students matriculate, these questions can evolve to parallel the increasingly complex texts and tasks that students encounter through the grades. That elaborate and comprehensive metacognition are necessary for success can be illustrated in relation to reading standards—in this case a second-grade English/Language Arts standard from the State of Texas:

> Reading/Comprehension of Literary Text/Fiction. Students understand, make inferences and draw conclusions about the structure and elements of fiction and provide evidence from text to support their understanding. Students are expected to: (A) describe similarities and differences in the plots and settings of several works by the same author; and (B) describe main characters in works of fiction, including their traits, motivations, and feelings. (*https://tea.texas.gov/sites/default/files/Grade2_TEKS_0817.pdf*)

A task analysis of this standard indicates that text comprehension is assumed or taken for granted as students engage in complex reading and reasoning. Clearly, this second-grade standard demands accomplished metacognition. It requires that students construct meaning from a story, which invokes second graders' fluency, vocabulary knowledge, comprehension strategies, and proficiency in phonics and decoding. In addition, readers must be able to manage their memory systems. They must call up prior knowledge from long-term memory related to plot and setting, and they must recall other stories by the same author. They must remember and characterize the traits and motivations of the main characters. As this information is recalled, students must work to use it within the limited space of working memory. Thus, readers must construct meaning, manage working memory and long-term memory, and conduct the numerous task-related processes. That this is a second-grade standard— the same grade as the student in the previous example who is working to develop metacognition to the point where he or she can manage reading and understanding simple stories—speaks volumes about both the need for metacognition and for instruction that fosters students' metacognitive ability.

A checklist that reflects the complexity and demands of the second-grade standard can complement previous simpler checklists. This practice follows the guideline that the ongoing teaching of metacognition "builds on preliminary and simple metacognitive routines" (Veenman et al., 2006, p. 9). As illustrated in the questions that follow, the next iteration of the metacognitive checklist and related instruction builds on the prior basic checklist questions (e.g., "Does that make sense?") and reflects increasing complexity and challenging standards. An elaborated comprehension checklist geared to the English/Language Arts second-grade standard could include the following questions:

- ☐ Have I understood the story?
- ☐ What do I already know about the author and the stories the author has written?
- ☐ Who are the main characters in the stories?
- ☐ What are their traits, motivations, and feelings?
- ☐ Does my response address all aspects of the standard?
- ☐ Did I understand the story?
- ☐ Do I understand all of the parts of this question?
- ☐ Did I use my prior knowledge about the plot, the setting, and the author?
- ☐ Can I characterize the traits and motivations of the main characters?
- ☐ Can I carefully manage all the tasks involved in this standard?

Note that such complex checklists can be divided into instructionally suitable "chunks" that best fit with the existing curriculum. According to the logic of standards and learning, over time, students working through such second-grade standards today will face increasingly complex reading challenges as they advance through the grades. As we teach readers, we will provide students with the necessary metacognitive mettle to meet those challenges.

The next example of a checklist takes us 10 school years forward in the lives of students and corresponds with a Common Core English/Language Arts Standard for informational text for grades 11 and 12. The checklist illustrates that although the demand for metacognition is consistent throughout students' school years, increasing the scope of student readers' metacognition is necessary. Here is an informational text standard for grades 11 and 12:

CC.11-12.R.I.8—Integration of Knowledge and Ideas: Delineate and evaluate the reasoning in seminal U.S. texts, including the application of constitutional principles and use of legal reasoning (e.g., in U.S. Supreme Court majority opinions and dissents) and the premises, purposes, and arguments in works of public advocacy (e.g., The Federalist, presidential addresses). *(www.corestandards. org/ELA-Literacy/RI/11-12/8)*

With this standard, comprehension of text is again assumed—indeed, it is seen as a starting point for students' analysis and evaluation of complex text. In addition to the analysis and evaluation of the reasoning used by authors of historical texts, students must have working knowledge of important legal and historical documents; they must be able to identify and evaluate the reasoning in seminal U.S. texts, including the application of constitutional principles and the use of legal reasoning (e.g., in U.S. Supreme Court majority opinions and dissents) and the premises, purposes, and arguments in works of public advocacy (e.g., the Federalist and presidential addresses). A suitable checklist, based on the foundation provided years earlier by the basic checklists created in elementary school, includes the following guiding metacognitive questions:

☐ What is my goal with this reading and assignment?

☐ Did I understand the texts?

☐ Do I understand all of the parts of this question?

☐ What do I already know about constitutional process and legal reasoning?

☐ Can I evaluate the reasoning used in the documents?

☐ Do the arguments used reflect constitutional principles and legal reasoning?

☐ Can I carefully manage all the tasks involved in this standard?

The metacognition required of students in a reading clinic or in second or twelfth grade is substantial. Becoming metacognitive is challenging, and our students' metacognitive abilities, like their cognitive abilities, develop as students mature. Under the proper conditions, the two types of abilities will develop concurrently. The continuous use of checklists from the early grades through high school, focused on the ever-increasingly complex texts and tasks that are expected of our students, again helps meet a central tenet of teaching readers metacognition—providing continuous models of metacognitive questions (Veenman et al., 2006), which over time can be internalized and then used independently by each student in varied reading situations.

Teaching readers in relation to metacognition is a challenging undertaking. I note that comprehension monitoring is important, but that viewing comprehension monitoring as "all that there is" to metacognition has potential drawbacks. Comprehension monitoring has a considerable reactive component—what a reader should do when a reading difficulty, such as an obstacle to meaning making, appears. Each of us experiences related comprehension-monitoring strategies and their power. We read merrily along until something is awry, and we are able to note that there is a problem. The determination that there is a problem is followed by the employment of "fix-it" strategies that address the problem. Comprehension monitoring helps us determine, identify, and fix problems that arise in the course of reading. Our ability to monitor comprehension is, of course, invaluable. Yet, it places a reactive (as opposed to proactive) notation on metacognition.

Proactive metacognition is as important and is reflected in the student behaviors of planning reading, setting goals, and appreciating all that comprises successful reading. The following checklist provides some examples:

☐ I gather my resources before I begin reading.

☐ I check on my prior knowledge for the topic of reading.

☐ I set my goal(s) for understanding the text.

☐ I set my goal(s) for any related tasks.

When metacognition is viewed more broadly, we also have the opportunity to appreciate its connection with reflective individuals, or students who possess self-knowledge and who know their place in the world in the best sense of that phrase. It's difficult to imagine creating checklist questions like "Do I appreciate the contributions that reading makes to my life?" and "Have I become a more self-assured reader as a result of being metacognitive?" Yet, these are the valuable insights of developing student readers that connect back to the metacognition that can be initiated by teaching readers and that begin with the self-awareness prompted by simple checklists and questions.

Research demonstrates the important role that metacognition plays in managing and informing cognitive strategies and processes that are necessary for school success. Thus determining the conditions in which metacognition can develop and thrive is a preeminent need. Teaching readers includes our efforts to "uncover" metacognitive thinking and metacognitive strategies, which are successful when we think aloud about metacognitive strategies and describe, model, and discuss their nature and uses. In essence, a goal of instruction is to make something that is invisible and valuable (metacognitive strategies), tangible and usable for students. Consider the following discussion, which is led by Maria, the teacher, and is focused on making metacognition accessible and understandable for Jamie, her student:

JAMIE: I don't know a lot of these words.

MARIA: When I use these metacognitive strategies they help me take control of my reading. They help me get to the small goals that lead to the big goal.

JAMIE: I'm not sure how to do that.

MARIA: OK. When I get to a point where there are lots of words that I don't know, I remind myself of things to do to stay on track. First, I'll stop reading to locate the things that need my attention—like an unfamiliar word.

JAMIE: Still not sure . . .

MARIA: Can you remember some of the reasons we might stop reading before we are finished?

JAMIE: 'Cause I don't understand.

MARIA: And once you stop because you don't understand, what can you do?

JAMIE: Oh, OK. I can read the part I don't understand. Read it again.

MARIA: Is it enough just to reread it? Will that do it for you? Will that solve the problem?

JAMIE: No! I am rereading to figure out what exactly is the problem. Where the meaning gets lost. Once I do that, I can start to try to fix it.

MARIA: Right! Remember, slowing down your reading can be a good thing, just like rereading. We slow down when we know we have to work to understand, and we reread when we think that we may not have gotten all that the text has to say.

Consider Maria's intent—to be supportive, to help Jamie avoid the negative associations with reading that may result from a lack of success, to keep the lesson moving along, to be friendly and helpful—all the while being focused on the helpful strategy of rereading to identify and fix a comprehension challenge. Thinking aloud allows teachers to describe the usefulness of strategies, when and where students might best use them, and the thinking behind them. Classroom scenarios are created to provide students with opportunities to learn and practice metacognitive thinking and related strategies. Effective metacognitive strategy instruction occurs in classrooms in which teachers encourage their students to be reflective and to develop the appropriate mindsets to engage with metacognition. This means that students must be invested in classroom learning and related tasks, that there must be clear goals, and that tasks present "doable" challenges.

TEACHING EXECUTIVE FUNCTIONING AND SELF-REGULATION

Executive functioning and self-regulation instruction are related to, but broader than, metacognition. Remember the working memory challenge: all of us work with limited brain space to succeed at reading. The difficult *broadpoint* paragraph illustrated this limitation. Helping students learn to best manage their resources—including constrained working memory—should be a priority.

Two successful approaches to executive functioning and self-regulation instruction focus on routines and explanations. Imagine undertaking school reading tasks without predictable and productive routines. A student would need to create, or learn anew, routines that have already been experienced each time school reading takes place. Healthy metacognitive routines require planning, time, and effort to become established—and our instruction and classroom environments should foster the development of routines. Routines for executive functioning and self-regulation provide students with predictability. The predictability affords our students practice with assigning their precious working memory resources to higher-order thinking and metacognition. In addition to our direct teaching of the concept of routine and demonstrating the steps in a routine, visual supports in the classroom that focus on steps in a procedure, such as problem solving, are helpful. Just as we expect that students will internalize and use the checklists that are introduced in print or digital form, we want them to internalize helpful routines, to learn to use them quickly and efficiently, to bring them toward automaticity, and to use them regularly. Routines also can be practiced to the point where they are conducted without consuming prohibitive amounts of students' attention and memory resources. Practice can make perfect (or close to perfect); it can also be somewhat automatic.

Executive functioning and self-regulation are central to students' success with challenging reading tasks and related projects. Ylvisaker and Feeney (1998) created the Goal–Plan–Do–Review model that students can use to improve their executive functioning. This model addresses Veenman and colleagues' (2006) recommendations that effective metacognition instruction involves explicit teaching that focuses on the value of metacognition and situates that instruction in authentic learning contexts. In its original form, the Goal–Plan–Do–Review is generic and accommodating of diverse human endeavors—it is useful in and out of the classroom for fostering executive functioning. The first step, "Goal," engages students by having them formulate and state a specific goal. Setting a goal, in turn, leads to "Plan," which requires that students develop the means to reach the goal they have formulated. This planning process involves identifying the materials necessary to proceed to the goal, the ordered procedural steps the students must take to reach the goal, and the time needed to reach the goal. In the "Plan" phase, students are increasingly expected to develop an awareness of their strengths and weaknesses, which in turn informs their selection of materials and the steps and time required. In the "Do" stage, students implement their plan. They work and monitor their progress toward the reading goal. Should monitoring indicate a problem, students are expected to determine the specific nature of the problem and propose and initiate a solution. The final step, "Review," requires that students focus on the questions "What worked?", "What didn't work?" and "What will I try differently next time?"

Consider elementary students who are designing and building a butterfly garden, and using the Goal–Plan–Do–Review approach. The scenario is one that requires them to read three texts (an Internet advice column sponsored by a botanical garden; a magazine article on "how to build gardens"; and a classroom text that describes flowers, insects, and their interactions) to determine what to include in the school's new butterfly garden. Using the Goal–Plan–Do–Review approach helps formalize students' steps as they address the set of texts and related tasks. Note how the following student work represents the placement of metacognition within the greater space of executive functioning:

> *Goals:* We want to learn about what plants and flowers attract butterflies, what plants and flowers grow well in our region, and how to build a garden.

Plan: We use the assignment to figure out the important things we must do. We will pair up and read the texts that focus on plants and flowers that attract butterflies and take notes related to how to build a butterfly garden.

Do: We read and used three text resources to identify and describe plants and flowers that attract butterflies. We took notes on the best plants and flowers. Next we figured out how much wood (for garden frames and raised beds) and soil we need to make the foundation for the garden. Then we looked at the height and width of the plants we determined to be best for the butterfly garden in our region. Next we approximated a cost for the wood, soil, and plants.

Review: We checked our work and findings against the goals we set at the beginning of the assignment. We created a written account of how we met those goals.

At the completion of the task students reviewed the goals, the plan, and their accomplishments. Students assessed their performance, determining what worked (or didn't work) and why. Students may also be in the position to consider how future, similar tasks can be approached efficiently. In effect, the Review questions helped students develop mindfulness, a state that combines the positive aspects of metacognition, self-regulation, and executive control. I note that because self-regulated learning is developmental, a Goal–Plan–Do–Review approach can be scaled in relation to each student's development stage, much like the metacognition checklists presented earlier in this chapter.

A perspective that focuses on both metacognition and executive functioning allows us to broaden our instruction related to becoming a mindful reader. For example, Pressley and Afflerbach (1995) determined that accomplished readers regularly used a broad variety of reflective, metacognitive routines. This diversity allows strong readers to attend to the array of metacognitive needs required of challenging readers. When the research findings on student executive functioning and metacognitive learning and practice are translated into classroom use, we can observe their sequential and detailed possibilities. Figure 7.1 can be read as a menu of suggestions for both the focus of our instruction and for the development of checklists that provide external prompts for students' metacognitive executive functioning and serve as models for later internalized prompts.

The importance of metacognition, executive functioning, and mindfulness—as goals of schooling and as the means for students to reach

Planning strategies

What are my specific goals for reading?

What resources do I need to meet my goals?

What procedures will help me meet my goals?

Monitoring strategies

Does that make sense?

How do I know?

Do I understand this?

Do I understand this well enough to use it in the required task?

How do I check my understanding in relation to the task at hand?

Fix-it strategies

When I encounter difficulties, what is my first step?

Can I locate the problem?

Can I remedy the problem?

Will rereading be helpful?

Will slowing down be helpful?

Evaluating strategies

Does my work meet the task demands?

Is my progress to this point aligned with my plan and standards?

What evidence can I use to make this determination?

How do I use this evidence?

Can I use a rubric to estimate the grade I will get from my performance?

Can I use the rubric to provide formative feedback during task performance and summative feedback upon the completion of the performance?

FIGURE 7.1. Executive functioning and self-assessment strategies: Posing questions. Adapted with permission from Pressley and Afflerbach (1995).

learning goals—is evident. We know that students must be aware, reflective, and mindful to succeed. Yet, these key aspects of reading development can be overlooked or treated as the serendipitous results of reading
instruction, instead of essential outcomes for which we plan and teach.
The idea that districts, schools, and classrooms are ready to take on the
demands of teaching metacognition and encouraging mindfulness for all
students is laudable. But is it realistic? Metacognition and mindfulness
are necessary for student success with all independent schoolwork, but
they are not a feature of many reading curricula.

Although metacognition is sometimes lost in the mix of hoped-for
learning outcomes, metacognition itself is specifically about cognition.
It is often thought of in relation to particular strategies and skills, as
students monitor and evaluate their progress at a reading task. This is all
well and good, as strategies and skills are clearly a "cognitive" for which
students should be metacognitive. Yet, there are important affective and
conative connections to metacognition. For example, how does motivation figure in a student's growth toward metacognition? What is the
nature of their relationship? Metacognition is ultimately about gaining
independence and agency with our work. As students advance toward
being fully metacognitive, how does their progress impact their self-
efficacy? How does it influence students' seeking or avoiding challenges?

Imagine the idea of gradual release of responsibility on a grand
scale—that our ultimate goal as effective teachers of readers is to transfer
not only strategies, but everything that students need to succeed and
be independent. If this goal is realized (and it is every time a student
succeeds independently at reading), we must make sure that students
have the tools and mindsets that promote success and independence.
Self-awareness and metacognition are at the center of these efforts. Consider the classrooms in which students are metacognitive and mindful
and use executive functioning. Yes, there is comprehension monitoring
and evaluation of progress in attaining near and far goals. There is also
an awareness of the individual in a social setting; some reflection on
accomplishments and challenges (and the ability to determine what contributed to them); a sense of self that feeds self-efficacy, and the ability to "see the big picture" of individual tasks, collaborative efforts, and
school in general. Once self-aware students gain such control and the
insights into their own performances, it is not surprising that they are
more accurate in the attributions they make for their performance, have
high self-efficacy, and are capable of independent work. Finally, student
learning about reflection, self-awareness, and comprehension monitoring

can transfer to other parts of the school day and to students' lives in general. The student who is aware of the connection between capability and reading outcomes strengthens his or her belief in the self as a reader, and the student who reflects on how team-based learning contributed to a superior class project understands the contributions of others and the benefits of teamwork.

ASSESSING METACOGNITION, EXECUTIVE FUNCTIONING, AND MINDFULNESS AS WE TEACH READERS

We want assessment to uncover students' metacognitive knowledge and strategies, to help us understand where in the process of becoming meta-cognitive readers our students stand, and to evaluate the effectiveness of our metacognitive instruction. At times, our assessment of metacognition, executive functioning, and mindfulness can be quick and accurate and be inferred when our students are reading independently and successfully. Indeed, this is the key goal of teaching readers and metacognition. However, because metacognition develops as students mature, we need assessments that provide reliable and valid information about students' progress at becoming metacognitive. Fortunately, there are numerous resources that focus on the assessment of metacognition, including classroom observations, teacher checklists, conversations with students, student journals and discussions, and exit cards. In addition, there are detailed metacognition assessment instruments, such as surveys and questionnaires, that can provide rich information on the status of students' metacognition.

What should be our focus as we assess readers' metacognition? The Metacognitive Awareness of Reading Strategies Inventory–Revised (MARSI-R; Mokhtari, Dimitrov, & Reichard, 2018; see Figure 7.2) examines the intersection of metacognition and cognitive strategies and contains items that can help guide our thinking about students' development. I recommend using items from the MARSI-R, because each item reminds me of important aspects of readers' metacognition. Thus any assessment of students' metacognition can use the MARSI-R itself or can "borrow" items to help create an assessment focus.

In addition to the information we obtain about students' performance by asking questions, students' actual reading performances are a rich source of metacognition information. For example, if we use reading inventories, Running Records, or miscue analysis, we can focus on

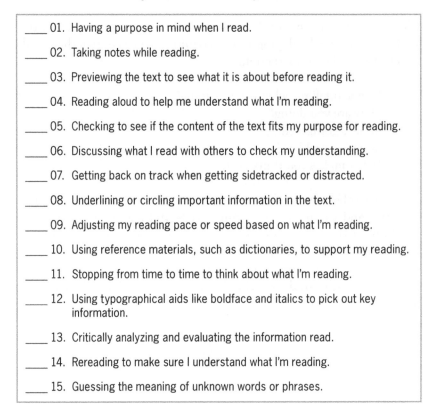

_____ 01. Having a purpose in mind when I read.

_____ 02. Taking notes while reading.

_____ 03. Previewing the text to see what it is about before reading it.

_____ 04. Reading aloud to help me understand what I'm reading.

_____ 05. Checking to see if the content of the text fits my purpose for reading.

_____ 06. Discussing what I read with others to check my understanding.

_____ 07. Getting back on track when getting sidetracked or distracted.

_____ 08. Underlining or circling important information in the text.

_____ 09. Adjusting my reading pace or speed based on what I'm reading.

_____ 10. Using reference materials, such as dictionaries, to support my reading.

_____ 11. Stopping from time to time to think about what I'm reading.

_____ 12. Using typographical aids like boldface and italics to pick out key information.

_____ 13. Critically analyzing and evaluating the information read.

_____ 14. Rereading to make sure I understand what I'm reading.

_____ 15. Guessing the meaning of unknown words or phrases.

FIGURE 7.2. Items from the Metacognitive Awareness of Reading Strategies Inventory–Revised (MARSI-R). Adapted with permission from Mokhtari, Dimitrov, and Reichard (2018).

comprehension-monitoring strategies used when students make miscues. A substitution that leads to considerable meaning change, and that is not noticed by the student reader, often signals that metacognition is not operating—or not operating at a level sufficient to note the miscue and address it. In other cases, students may exhibit continuous use of metacognitive attention and strategies. That self-corrections (a strong indicator that students are metacognitive) are not considered errors or miscues when we analyze students' oral reading illustrates the importance assigned to metacognition.

Along with assessment tools like reading inventories, our teacher questioning can help us uncover and best understand the nature of students' metacognitive development. For example, the following questions, when asked as students read, can contribute to our determination that students continue developing as metacognitive readers or that they would benefit from related instruction:

- Can you tell me what you are doing?
- How are you doing?
- What's going well?
- What's a problem?
- What makes you think that?

We best help our students when we are able to identify specific meta-cognitive and executive functioning needs and address them with tar-geted instruction. Regarding assessment, broad coverage of the different aspects of students' development will position us to best focus on the sta-tus of students' metacognition, executive functioning, and mindfulness. Over the course of students' school careers, we are helping them become self-sufficient and successful.

(CHAPTER REVIEW)

1. Explain how metacognition helps students develop into independent and successful readers.

2. How can checklists contribute to students' emerging metacognition and executive functioning?

3. How can metacognition, executive functioning, and mindfulness influence students' motivation to read?

4. How can teachers' questions help young readers establish comprehension-monitoring routines?

(CHAPTER 8)

Self-Efficacy

Clearly, it is not simply a matter of how capable you are;
it is also a matter of how capable you believe you are.

—FRANK PAJARES

Do our students approach reading believing that they can succeed? Do they perceive themselves to be in control of their reading? Do our students take credit for their success, take the initiative when there are challenges, and take responsibility for improving? Does students' positive motivation to read follow from their high self-efficacy? If the answers to all these questions are "Yes," then we are doing well in helping students develop self-efficacy. We are teaching readers. If the answers are "No," our students may not be prepared to become better readers or to take on increasingly complex reading texts and tasks. In this chapter, I focus on developing self-efficacy, as we help students experience success and focus on the connections between their capabilities and that success. Bandura (1986) describes self-efficacy as follows: "Self-efficacy refers to an individual's belief in his or her capacity to execute behaviors necessary to produce specific performance attainments."[1] In the classroom, this translates to the kindergartner listening intently and participating in discussion after a read-aloud and to the second grader believing that she will succeed in understanding the new science book. It translates to the confident fifth grader critiquing a poem, and the middle schooler knowing he has the knowledge and motivation to read like a historian. It means that the enthusiasm for reading and learning that so many students bring to school is never lost, but furthered by creating classrooms where their accomplishments are noted and celebrated.

---

[1] Retrieved from *www.apa.org/pi/aids/resources/education/self-efficacy.aspx*.

Our students' self-efficacy is reflected in their belief in themselves as readers. Based on this belief, students approach the texts and tasks of reading with a "can-do" attitude. The "can-do" belief is not a given for all of our students; it is nourished by a history of successful reading that provides the foundation for understanding themselves as capable readers. It is important in developing self-efficacy that students establish a connection between reading and succeeding, and they must give themselves credit for their success. As I hope will become apparent, self-efficacy is at the heart of much human success, and a lack of self-efficacy is deeprooted in failure. Bandura (2006) further states:

> Among the mechanisms of human agency, none is more central or pervasive than belief of personal efficacy. *Unless people believe they can produce desired effects by their actions, they have little incentive to act, or to persevere in the face of difficulties.* Whatever other factors serve as guides and motivators, they are rooted in the core belief that one has the power to effect changes by one's actions. [italics added] (p. 165)

It bears repeating that our student readers are not simply strategy and skill users. They will use strategies and skills when they believe that they are in control of learning, that using strategies and skills is worthwhile, and that their learning goals are attainable. How many of our struggling readers don't believe that they can, in Bandura's words, "produce desired effects by their actions," be it using phonics to decode words, reading fluently, determining the meaning of words, or understanding a simple written story? If the desired outcomes of school reading include understanding, participating, and not failing, what results from a student's history of not understanding, not participating, and failing?

SAMPLING THE SCIENCE

Self-efficacy is reflected in our beliefs that we are capable of carrying out actions to achieve goals: "Self-efficacy refers to people's judgements about their capability to perform particular tasks. Task-related self-efficacy increases the effort and persistence towards challenging tasks; therefore, increasing the likelihood that they will be completed" (Barling &

Beattie, 1983, as cited in Axtell & Parker, 2003, p. 114). Research tells us that individuals with high self-efficacy are more likely to persevere when faced with difficulties, are more inclined to perceive a difficult situation as a challenge, and are less affected by setbacks or failure than individuals with low self-efficacy (Bandura, 2006). In contrast, Carroll and Fox (2017) note that students "who perform unsuccessfully may do so, not because they lack the skills and knowledge, but because they lack the efficacy beliefs to use them well" (pp. 20–21).

The research base on self-efficacy is extensive and is not limited to reading. We know that students with low self-efficacy often adopt a performance orientation toward reading: they are more concerned about how they appear as readers to their teachers and classmates than on comprehending and learning from text (Walker, 2003). These students also make erroneous attributions for their performance, away from effort and toward luck and task difficulty. These attributions further reduce students' motivation. In addition, students with low self-efficacy have low self-regulation and limited metacognition—a tendency not to reflect on aspects of reading that include making progress toward goals. From a struggling student's perspective, this makes sense: Why invest time and effort in an enterprise for which you anticipate failure? Low self-efficacy can lead students to task avoidance as well (Bandura, 1994). Prior reading experiences can create low self-efficacy for reading, as students develop the expectation that they will not succeed, not enjoy reading, or not reach their reading goals. We shouldn't be surprised when these students develop strategies to avoid reading.

In comparison, students with high self-efficacy are focused on managing their reading—setting goals, measuring ongoing progress toward attaining those goals, monitoring comprehension, and evaluating their work. Students who believe they can be successful in an activity are more likely to engage in it (Carroll & Fox, 2017; Schunk and Zimmerman, 1997). These students are invested in the idea that they are readers, and that they can succeed.

Students' self-efficacy influences their effort given during reading, their performance in reading-related activity, and their overall reading achievement (Henk and Melnick, 1995). For example, self-efficacy contributes to children's fluency development (Peura et al., 2019). Yang, Badri, Al Rashedi, and Almazrouhi (2018) "affirm the important contributions of student self-efficacy, extrinsic motivation, and home literacy environment to reading achievement" (p. 1).

A child who tries to read a moderately difficult book and succeeds (thereby increasing self-efficacy) is more likely to try to attempt a similar task in the future. Similarly, students who read in accordance with their ability often increase their self-efficacy (Bandura, 2006; Guthrie & Wigfield, 1997), while students who struggle regularly with reading will not. Guthrie and Wigfield (1997) and Zimmerman (2000) have examined the influence of students' belief in their own reading abilities and found that students with low-reading self-efficacy avoided challenging reading activities and withdrew from tasks they perceived as too difficult. The connection between self-efficacy and school achievement gets stronger as students grow older. By the time they are in high school, their self-efficacy beliefs may be as strongly related to their success than any measure of their academic ability, including reading achievement level. Clearly, fostering students' self-efficacy should be a central feature of teaching readers.

Research documents the conditions and opportunities that promote the development of students' self-efficacy and describes the major influences on self-efficacy: mastery experiences, modeling, feedback, and emotional and physical experiences. Bandura (2006) proposed that the most direct and effective means for helping students build self-efficacy is *mastery experiences.* "Nothing succeeds like success," is an often-used aphorism, and I use it as a guiding thought in developing mastery experiences for students that contribute to self-efficacy. Understanding a story, discussing a science blog with classmates, answering a teacher's question correctly, and realizing that one is learning and growing are all instances in which mastery experiences can build self-efficacy.

We can tell our students that they are successful, and we can examine and explore the lives of successful people. Yet, the mastery experience of success in reading has a direct influence on students' reading self-efficacy. In fact, the primary influence on students' self-efficacy beliefs is actual success in completing challenging academic tasks (Pajares, 2005). The need for our students' positive reading experiences is obvious here; we cannot expect self-efficacy to develop when challenge and effort do not result in success and accomplishment. Although mastery experiences fuel self-efficacy, we must also focus on fostering students' persistence and effort. Not all reading is effortless, and not every act of reading is immediately rewarding. Helping students "build in" the ideas that even accomplished adult readers face challenges can aid the development of persistence and the giving of effort, while contributing to self-efficacy.

Resilience leads students to understand that success in reading may involve time, effort, and repeated attempts at constructing meaning. It works against the simplistic notion that good readers read effortlessly and experience success all the time.

A second approach to helping our student readers develop self-efficacy involves providing them *models of self-efficacy*. According to Bandura (1994), "Seeing people similar to oneself succeed by sustained effort raises observers' beliefs that they too possess the capabilities to master comparable activities to succeed" (p. 72). Models can help students make the connections between effort and successful outcomes of their reading. A classroom focus on reading accomplishments—ours and our students'—accompanied by accounts of the reading challenges we face, the means used to address and overcome these challenges, and an explicit linking of these accomplishments can help students best understand the value of self-efficacy and the processes by which it is developed. As teachers, we can describe our own initial failure to understand directions for assembling a piece of furniture or to successfully navigate an Internet text, followed by an account of how we eventually understood what needed to be done and succeeded. Of course, the more relatable the accomplishments and the challenges faced in overcoming them, the more potential value these models and lessons hold for our students.

A further influence on the development of student readers' self-efficacy is *feedback*, or the spoken, written, or sometimes nonverbal communication given students by teachers and classmates. Bandura asserted that people could be persuaded to believe that they have the skills and capabilities to succeed and that feedback can provide the convincing narrative. Feedback that focuses on the quality of reading or on the effort given to reading can lead students to view themselves as either talented or needy readers.

Consider a time when someone said something positive and encouraging that helped you achieve a goal, be it academic, social, athletic, or something else. Well-timed and well-placed positive feedback can work wonders. I remember a 10K race several years ago for which I did absolutely no training or warm-up, and the mighty struggle I found in trying to crest the final hill in the race. Each step was painful, and with my head down I was talking myself into stopping. A man standing in his front yard said, "You got this. You're going to make it." I looked up with a smile that said, "Thank you," and pressed on. The man's feedback immediately changed my perspective and helped me finish. How powerful a few choice words can be! Verbal encouragement from others helps us overcome self-doubt and can influence our willingness to persist and maintain focus. We sometimes internalize the voices of others, and when we do so we can urge ourselves to succeed. Words of encouragement also help us focus on things that are going well and on things that turn out well.

Of course, students' *emotional and physical experiences* influence self-efficacy. Students' reactions to these experiences accumulate with time, and they are shaped by histories of success or failure at reading. With mastery experiences, we can expect that students' emotions and feelings reflect success and contribute to a positive attitude about reading. With consistent experience that does not involve mastery, we can expect that students who are stressed, who become anxious at the mention of reading, or who are surrounded by negative emotions often dwell on these factors in relation to their reading performance. Recall Betts's (1940) observation from Chapter 4:

> As the typical pupil becomes increasingly frustrated, he may exhibit tension, movements of the body, hands, and feet, he may frown and squint, and he may exhibit other types of emotional behavior characteristic of a frustrated individual. (p. 741)

The effects of these emotions and reactions on students' reading development should not be underestimated. In such situations, student readers' frustration and anxiety are an obstacle to developing self-efficacy. Healthy development of self-efficacy may involve helping students learn to minimize the negative effects—in effect, acknowledging the presence of these factors, but developing coping mechanisms to deal with them. Emotional and physical experiences relate, first and foremost, to students' reading performance, which involves their perception and memory of prior reading experiences related to the degree of success or failure. Student readers' self-efficacy is further influenced by their physiological states. These represent emotions and feelings that students experience as they read. Both can accumulate with time and are influenced by repeated success or failure.

To summarize, students' self-efficacy develops in relation to their actions and thoughts and to the environments in which they read. Success in reading breeds future success: accomplished student readers believe that they can succeed. Readers with low self-efficacy may be hard-pressed to become successful; believing that they are not strong readers, they avoid reading when they can. Such avoidance greatly diminishes opportunities for these students to learn and practice reading strategies and skills. Another result is that they do not identify as readers, fall further behind, and may lack both the skill and will to succeed. Each of the four factors that influence student readers' self-efficacy—mastery experiences, modeling, feedback, and emotional and physical experiences—can be directly addressed in classrooms. The factors can be combined as well to further empower student self-efficacy.

TEACHING READERS: SELF-EFFICACY IN THE CLASSROOM

Healthy classroom environments provide mastery experiences, modeling, feedback, and emotional and physical experiences to help foster students' self-efficacy development. Effective teachers draw from each of these four bases to develop and deliver instruction. In this section, I discuss two students who have different levels of self-efficacy and how the self-efficacy of each student develops and operates in the classroom. Consider Alicia and Henry, one student with a history of success with reading and one with a history of reading struggles. Alicia grew up with books. Her parents took turns reading nightly to her and then with her. Her family created a home library of books on topics that interested Alicia and that were geared to her developing reading ability and anticipated her future reading ability. Her parents were available to read with her, and they celebrated her attempts to read. There was no pressure on Alicia to read perfectly—her family wanted, first and foremost, to instill a joy of reading. She was read stories, she reread with help from her parents, and then successfully read on her own. She provided the narratives for wordless picture books. A software program and laptop computer helped her develop an understanding of letters and sounds and of their relationships. Her parents encouraged her reading.

As her reading was developing, her self-efficacy was growing by leaps and bounds. In effect, Alicia's self-efficacy was nurtured through mastery experiences, modeling, feedback, and emotional and physical experiences. At every turn, reading presented itself as something to be enjoyed and as something to succeed at. This fortunate situation resulted in Alicia having early success with attempts to read simple storybooks. Reading was an activity she wanted to do, and her early experiences supported her. Her attempts at reading were accompanied by her parents' praise. They pointed out what Alicia was doing well—and encouraged her to always give effort. During her early years, Alicia's experiences with reading helped her build a connection between the things she did as an early reader, her efforts, and reading success. Alicia's emotions related to reading were strong and positive. Under these conditions, her self-efficacy developed easily. Alicia identifies as a reader, and reading is at the center of her social and academic lives. Teaching readers, in Alicia's case, involves maintaining the series of reading successes on which her accomplished reading is based and making sure that her self-efficacy is sufficient for each new reading challenge during the school year.

In contrast, a classmate, Henry, did not have the privilege of growing up with books. There were few books in the home, and they were not of interest to him because they were not on an accessible reading level. The community library was a long bus ride away, and there was little time to visit. Reading was not modeled at home, and his parents had few resources to purchase books or pay for online subscriptions. Based on his limited home reading experiences, Henry started school with an interest in reading, but few emergent reading skills. Reading was effortful from the start, and his struggles were often in the spotlight as a member of the low-ability reading group. Grade-level texts were not Henry-level texts. Henry's successful experiences with reading were few and far between. The instructional focus in Henry's reading group did not include attention to metacognition or mindfulness, and he reached the end of kindergarten without a history of reading and succeeding. Henry has not developed an understanding of himself as a reader who could succeed. Reading instruction that focuses on the mechanics of reading provides for occasional successes with worksheets, but Henry is not in the habit of succeeding when reading stories. His self-efficacy is shaky, as is his belief in himself. As much as Alicia identifies as a reader, Henry does not.

These accounts of Henry and Alicia can be viewed through a cognitive lens—and our perception would be that Alicia is thriving and Henry is struggling. Henry clearly needs to bolster his reading strategies and skills. But our observation cannot stop there. If we view both students through the lens of self-efficacy, we see two very different realities. Alicia has had many opportunities to succeed at reading in learning environments that support her efforts. Her parents and teachers focus on mindfulness to help her make the connection between her work and success at that work. Alicia identifies as a reader and already has a history of succeeding along with accompanying high self-efficacy. She believes in herself as a reader.

Henry's situation is starkly different. A reading diagnostic plan based on Henry's cognitive performance includes repeated teaching of the strategies he needs to decode, read fluently, and construct meaning. As much as this learning is difficult for Henry, the challenge is compounded by a lack of self-efficacy, which, in effect, undermines Henry's efforts to become a better reader before he starts. It is imperative that Henry's diagnostic plan—focused exclusively on cognitive strategies and skills—be expanded to address the dire need for him to begin to build self-efficacy in reading. In other words, Henry needs experiences within which reading and success coexist. He needs to " . . . believe he can produce desired effects" (Bandura, 2006, p. 165) when he reads. Ms. Falcek, Henry and Alicia's teacher, works with colleagues to develop instruction that focuses on self-efficacy.

Ms. Falcek constructs classroom tasks, environments, and situations that help foster Henry's self-efficacy and sustain Alicia's self-efficacy. Ms. Falcek's work in the course of the school year is informed by the research that describes the positive effects of mastery experiences, modeling, feedback, and emotional and physical experiences. She aims to both foster students' competence and confidence and to challenge their underconfidence when possible. Finally, Ms. Falcek is keen on creating classroom situations in which students can generalize positive self-efficacy beliefs.

Mastery Experiences

In relation to mastery experiences, Ms. Falcek maintains a large classroom library—replete with books, articles, and Internet reading that respect and meet every student's interests (and so, prior knowledge), motivations, and strategy and skill levels. Because her students are motivated, reading in areas of interest to them and best matched in terms of text complexity, self-efficacy has the best chance to take root with Henry and to continue to flourish with Alicia. Ms. Falcek embraces the idea that "nothing succeeds like success," and she has devoted significant portions of the reading day to helping her students experience success and thus build self-efficacy. Although mastery experiences are enhanced by the diverse library collection, Ms. Falcek knows that providing books is not sufficient for some readers. Alicia, for example, readily reads and succeeds with books that she chooses from the classroom collection, but Henry must be led to books whose topics interest him. Part of Ms. Falcek's instructional plan is driven by the goal of steering Henry toward, and not away from, books and reading.

The greatest challenges to mastery experiences for Henry reside in content-area reading, where he must read and be responsible for learning.

It is challenging to have readers who are efficacious in one area and but not in others. To these ends, Ms. Falcek scaffolds from Henry's interested attempts to read about motocross bike racing to science and social studies.

> MS. FALCEK: What do you do when you encounter a new word in reading about motocross?
>
> HENRY: If it's important enough, I'll ask a friend or you. Or look it up.
>
> MS. FALCEK: Well, how about you try that here in social studies?

The tasks we ask children to perform in relation to reading are of similar concern, and they receive similar attention. From Ms. Falcek's perspective, reading requires that students comprehend a text and then are able to use what is comprehended in meaningful tasks. Thus mastery experiences include both texts with which all students can experience success and text-related tasks that are attainable. For example, her students are encouraged to "read like historians," seeking out and reading source texts, determining their origin, and then evaluating them for accuracy and trustworthiness. At a minimum, students must be able to construct an understanding of each text and then use a suite of strategies that help them meet the "reading-like-historians" tasks. The history texts selected are within the reach of elementary students' comprehension strategies, and they include diary entries, advertisements, and newspaper articles from different historical eras. The related tasks, such as evaluating texts for the legitimacy of a claim made and the evidence provided to support it, are also chosen and sequenced so that they are within the reach of each student. A result is the accumulation of student success experiences, which continually feed the development of self-efficacy.

Modeling

Ms. Falcek also asks Henry to talk with her about other areas and tasks in which he does well—knowing where and when he is efficacious can help direct his thinking and his efforts, as well as remind him that he regularly experiences success. Here, the capacity for self-efficacy is within Henry but is removed from his reading challenges. As she models reading comprehension strategies, she also models enthusiasm and self-efficacy—she discusses her interactions with the text and how she is meeting reading challenges as they arise. She consistently explains how her belief that she will succeed and her past small successes contribute to her effort and pride and motivate her. She reminds Henry that he is successful in both motocross and skateboarding and encourages him to think about how his success in these sports is achieved. Part of this effort is intended to help Henry create an interior dialogue focused on believing in himself as a reader.

Ms. Falcek's classroom library is filled with books that tell the stories of challenges and overcoming them, and these books provide support for self-efficacy. A reason to celebrate *Rosa* by Nikki Giovanni or *The Little Engine That Could* is that these stories provide models of believing in one's self, of overcoming obstacles, and of succeeding. Further, if we have the luxury of having real or virtual author visits to our classrooms, in which many drafts of a single story are shared with students, teachers and authors are providing a model of the work and effort that go into a job well done. This modeling can help students understand that single instances and efforts may not be where to look for mastery and success—rather applying effort and attention over time can lead to a mastery experience. The biographies of civic and spiritual leaders, athletes, and artists also serve as models of self-efficacy and can help students learn about how self-efficacy develops in concert with effort and applying one's self.

For Henry, a key section of the library contains stories of athletes who overcome immense challenges related to their health, their talent, and racism. Henry's keen interest in and familiarity with sports places him in a good position to want to read about sports and to believe that he can succeed—to be both motivated and efficacious. The stories also tell the tale of efficacy developed over time—not instantaneously, but emerging as the result of people believing in and applying themselves and ultimately experiencing success.

Feedback

Henry so needs to be reinforced for his increasing efforts at reading and for his successes. At home, Henry's mother is supportive of his schoolwork and Henry knows that he is supported, but because her feedback is not text or task specific, it does not help him make connections between his effort and the outcomes of his work. In contrast, Ms. Falcek creates classroom routines that provide texts and reading-related tasks that are accessible for Henry. His good work results in specific praise that helps him reference specific instances to make the connection between feed-back and his success. Ms. Falcek is guided by two general thoughts: to praise what is praiseworthy and to praise effort and persistence. With respect to Alicia, her feedback is regularly focused on work well done, although Alicia appears to be on autopilot with her self-efficacy and self-assuredness as a reader.

Bandura (2006) believes that self-efficacy can flourish when students are persuaded to believe in their ability to succeed. Consistent feedback on Alicia's and Henry's reading performances that is accurate, truthful, and focused on what is being accomplished works here. When students have the skills and capabilities to succeed, our feedback provides the narrative to connect work with success.

As we strive to create exemplary classroom environments, one aspect relates to how and when students experience their peers' work and accomplishments. Do our students share their successes, and are they celebrated? Are the means for all students' successes discussed and made clear? Are successes shared so that there are increased opportunities to understand how students have some control over their learning? Having the effort, learning, and success connections made visible, especially with peers, makes possible vicarious learning related to self-efficacy. However, evoking the potential power of vicarious experience to develop self-efficacy comes with the caveat that results may be positive or negative. A classroom marked by competition and individual performance may result in vicarious models being received differently than in classrooms where cooperation or collaboration prevail. Social modeling can help students develop self-efficacy. Witnessing other people success-fully completing a task is another important source for encouraging all students' self-efficacy. Finally, when students are able to reflect on their own work, they are in the position to use their accomplishments as a self-efficacious model of success.

Emotional and Physical Experiences

Part of Ms. Falcek's plan is based on understanding Henry's prior emotional and physical experiences related to reading and efficacy. Discussions with teaching colleagues help her understand his past history and the situations in which self-doubt typically shows itself. Henry's reading is always influenced by his perception and memory of prior experiences of success or failure. He is in the habit of not reflecting on and of not being mindful about his reading because he does not want to dwell on unhappy things. To counter this habit, Ms. Falcek's understanding of Henry's love of sports and his accomplishments as a developing athlete informs her work of connecting Henry with texts and tasks that are related to positive emotions.

The goal for Henry is to believe in himself as a successful reader. These tasks necessarily require focused attention and effort on his part, both of which have been absent in what he brings to reading in school. Ms. Falcek plans instruction to meet both daily and long-term goals. How can Henry experience success each day in reading? How can this be an "earned" rather than a shallow success? How can the series of positive experiences with reading lead to a change in Henry's self-efficacy?

In summary, students' reading success breeds self-efficacy, and self-efficacy equips students to continue striving for reading success. Lack of self-efficacy can have a debilitating effect on student mindsets and on their reading performance. We are fortunate to have voluminous research that describes the nature and power of self-efficacy in reading, and there are several paths that can lead students to increased self-efficacy and reading success. Classrooms that focus on mastery experiences, modeling, feedback, and physical and emotional experiences are healthy environments for generating self-efficacy. Students may possess reading strategies and skills, but the use of these cognitive tools depends, in part, on our student readers' beliefs that doing so will be worth the effort and that they will succeed.

ASSESSING SELF-EFFICACY AS WE TEACH READERS

We are fortunate to have an array of assessments that can provide detailed information on the state of students' self-efficacy. To begin with, self-efficacy often "shows itself," so our observations of students as they read and go through the school day are a potentially rich source of useful assessment information. Children with established strategies and skills are likely to be aware that they are good at reading and therefore have a higher self-efficacy (Morgan and Fuchs, 2007). As described earlier in this chapter, students with high self-efficacy often exhibit motivation, persistence at a task, and a belief in self. Struggling readers lack persistence and giving effort because they do not believe them to be worth their while. It follows that if an assessment goal is to identify those students most in need of help in developing self-efficacy, our observations of students who are reluctant readers can be a helpful first step. Conversations with students that are focused on their reporting of their reading experiences in and out of school can also inform us about self-efficacy. We can also refer to our existing reading assessments. For example, the research finding that students with low test scores tend to have low self-efficacy suggests that our struggling readers would benefit from determining the nature of their self-efficacy.

Ms. Falcek believes that observing and listening to her students provides valuable information regarding their self-efficacy. In addition to her habit of looking and listening in relation to students' classroom performances and verbalizations, she uses items from the Reading Self-Efficacy Questionnaire (RS-EQ; Carroll & Fox, 2017) to assess her students' reading self-efficacy. Students are asked to respond to 22 items (see Figure 8.1), each describing a specific classroom reading task (e.g., Read out loud in front of the class). Students indicate their beliefs about what they can (and cannot) do by indicating where they are positioned on a 7-point continuum.

Similar items can be found in the Myself As A Learner scale (MALS; Burden, 2012), which focuses on students' general academic self-concepts, and the Children's Perceived Self-Efficacy (CPSE; Bandura, 1990) scale, which assesses self-efficacy in a wide range of academic, social, and leisure contexts. Finally, the Self-Efficacy for Learning Form (SELF; Zimmerman, Kitsantas, and Campillo, 2005) focuses on specific classroom reading tasks and asks students to report the probability that they would (or would not) be able to do particular tasks. Sample items from the SELF include:

- When you notice you are having trouble concentrating on a reading assignment, can you refocus your attention and learn the material?
- When you don't understand a paragraph you have just read, can you clarify it by careful rereading?
- When you have trouble recalling key facts in a reading assignment, can you find a way to remember all of them 2 weeks later?
- When you have trouble remembering complex definitions from a textbook, can you redefine them so that you will recall them?
- When you are given an extensive reading assignment to cover before class the next day, can you set aside enough time in your schedule to finish it?

Read each sentence and rate how certain YOU are that you can do the things described below. It is important you tell us what YOU think about your reading. When you think about reading, think about any reading that you do at school and at home. These could be things you read in books, magazines, newspapers, comics, emails, text messages, and the Internet. To give an answer, circle one of the numbers on the scale below the item.

1. Read out loud in front of the class
   Very certain I cannot do 1   2   3   4   5   6   7 Very certain I can do

2. Continue reading even when I find it difficult
   Very certain I cannot do 1   2   3   4   5   6   7 Very certain I can do

3. Work out the sounds in words I have not seen before
   Very certain I cannot do 1   2   3   4   5   6   7 Very certain I can do

4. Read out loud in front of the class
   Very certain I cannot do 1   2   3   4   5   6   7 Very certain I can do

5. Continue reading even when I find it difficult
   Very certain I cannot do 1   2   3   4   5   6   7 Very certain I can do

6. Work out the sounds in words I have not seen before
   Very certain I cannot do 1   2   3   4   5   6   7 Very certain I can do

7. Sound out a word that I find hard to read
   Very certain I cannot do 1   2   3   4   5   6   7 Very certain I can do

8. Read on my own without an adult's help
   Very certain I cannot do 1   2   3   4   5   6   7 Very certain I can do

9. Read things that are harder than the book I normally read at school
   Very certain I cannot do 1   2   3   4   5   6   7 Very certain I can do

10. Know what I can do to improve my reading
    Very certain I cannot do 1   2   3   4   5   6   7 Very certain I can do

11. Continue reading even when I find the subject boring
    Very certain I cannot do 1   2   3   4   5   6   7 Very certain I can do

12. Read out loud quickly and still get words right
    Very certain I cannot do 1   2   3   4   5   6   7 Very certain I can do

(continued)

FIGURE 8.1. Reading Self-Efficacy Questionnaire. Reprinted with permission from Carroll and Fox (2017).

13. Make out words easily when I read
Very certain I cannot do 1   2   3   4   5   6   7 Very certain I can do

14. Improve my reading if I really want to
Very certain I cannot do 1   2   3   4   5   6   7 Very certain I can do

15. Continue reading even when I do not like the subject
Very certain I cannot do 1   2   3   4   5   6   7 Very certain I can do

16. Read as well as my friends
Very certain I cannot do 1   2   3   4   5   6   7 Very certain I can do

17. Continue reading even when I get frustrated
Very certain I cannot do 1   2   3   4   5   6   7 Very certain I can do

18. Practice reading in my spare time even when I don't have to
Very certain I cannot do 1   2   3   4   5   6   7 Very certain I can do

19. Read without making lots of mistakes
Very certain I cannot do 1   2   3   4   5   6   7 Very certain I can do

20. Read difficult books
Very certain I cannot do 1   2   3   4   5   6   7 Very certain I can do

21. Read a book I have not read before
Very certain I cannot do 1   2   3   4   5   6   7 Very certain I can do

22. Work out the sounds in words I have not seen before
Very certain I cannot do 1   2   3   4   5   6   7 Very certain I can do

FIGURE 8.1. (continued)

Clearly, we are not wanting for a variety of self-efficacy assessment opportunities. As with assessments of metacognition and motivation (and of skill and strategy), it is challenging to administer to an entire class the full set of questions in any of these surveys and questionnaires. Trying out individual questions to determine the type and value of the responses they elicit is a fruitful practice, and when this approach is combined with other sources of information about self-efficacy, including classroom observations and student interviews, we can determine each student's self-efficacy growth.

(CHAPTER REVIEW)

1. Give a detailed example of each of the four influences on students' self-efficacy development: mastery experiences, modeling, feedback, and emotional and physical experiences.

2. How can high self-efficacy contribute to our student readers' reading development and reading achievement?

3. Explain how otherwise competent readers do not do well if they have low self-efficacy.

4. Describe how self-efficacy can have positive or negative effects on students' motivation to read.

5. Imagine that you are observing a student with low self-efficacy. What would you see?

CHAPTER 9

Motivation and Engagement

Motivation and engagement do not constitute a "warm and fuzzy"
extra component of efforts to improve literacy. These interrelated
elements are a primary vehicle for improving literacy.
—IRVIN, MELTZER, AND DUKES (2007, p. 31)

Motivation and engagement are key factors in teaching readers. Motivated and engaged readers are characterized by enthusiasm, focus, attention, and accomplishment. In classrooms, these readers gravitate to situations that feature reading, which leads to more practice and learning. Motivated and engaged students assign a high value to reading, appreciating how it serves to inform, entertain, and persuade. These students identify as readers; indeed, this part of their personalities encourages further reading. In this chapter we examine motivation and engagement, the relationship between them, and how to foster both factors in our reading classrooms.

Motivation and engagement influence both reading development and reading achievement. The role of motivation and engagement in human learning is documented across decades of research, and it has been a focus of high-quality teaching for millennia. In fact, it is impossible to imagine effective teaching if students' motivation and engagement are lacking. Motivation supports students' attention and effort as they develop as readers, while engagement reflects "the quality of students' participation with learning activities" (Skinner, Kindermann, & Furrer, 2009, p. 494). Engaging classroom environments provide motivation for students to be strategic and enhance their reading development. Motivated readers give time and effort when they are reading both in and out of school (Afflerbach et al., 2013; Alexander, 2003). In contrast, struggling student readers are often hindered by a lack of motivation and related engagement, putting them at a decided disadvantage, because without motivation and engagement, students' attention, perseverance, and learning opportunities are limited.

We often find the words *motivation* and *engagement* used together. Merriam-Webster defines motivation as "a motivating force, stimulus, or influence" (*www.merriam-webster.com/dictionary/motivation*). Irvin et al. (2007) describe the importance of engagement:

> Motivating students is important—without it, teachers have no point of entry. But it is *engagement* that is critical, because the level of engagement over time is the vehicle through which classroom instruction influences student outcomes.

Engaged reading represents "a merger of motivation and thoughtfulness," and engaged readers are "mastery oriented, intrinsically motivated, and have self-efficacy" (Guthrie and Klauda, 2014, p. 388). Our classroom observations reflect how research describes engaged readers: they find reading pleasurable and rewarding, they have high self-efficacy and are confident, and they put effort into their reading when needed. Motivation is an essential mindset (Dweck, 1986) with which students approach and engage in reading, and motivation and engagement contribute to both reading development and reading achievement.

The relationship between motivation and engagement is characterized by reciprocity: Engagement influences motivation, and vice versa (Afflerbach, 2016). As already noted, the motivated student reader expects to be engaged with reading in school and out. In turn, engagement optimizes students' experiences and achievements with reading, adding to their positive reading experiences. Students who have experienced success in reading look forward to reading and they are motivated to read more. There is a contrasting reciprocity for struggling readers: a lack of motivation to read is an obstacle to engagement, and without engagement students' reading experiences are compromised. Disengagement leads to lowered motivation for future reading. Students' histories with reading influence motivation and engagement.

Equally important is the fact that students' ongoing reading experiences matter. Students who are motivated to read, but who must participate in school reading that they consider boring, irrelevant, or useless may approach subsequent reading tasks with lessened motivation. In effect, they may learn to be less engaged, hampering learning. When texts and reading assignments lead students to question the value of what is read, future motivation and engagement are at risk. A motivated but suddenly disengaged reader may struggle to maintain future motivation. Further, readers who experience failure or embarrassment while reading in school may experience lower motivation and become less engaged. In contrast, a reluctant reader who experiences engaging reading and related tasks may gain in motivation for future reading.

SAMPLING THE SCIENCE

Motivation to read, according to Conradi, Jang, and McKenna (2014) is "the drive to read resulting from a comprehensive set of an individual's beliefs about, attitudes towards, and goals for reading" (p. 156). Thus motivation can guide our students' reading behaviors and actions (Eccles & Wigfield, 2002), with strong consequences for reading development:

> The benefits of motivation for achievement growth are not a mere marginal luxury. Reading motivation may stand as the strongest psychological variable influencing achievement. (Guthrie & Klauda, 2015, p. 48)

The influence of reading instruction on students' reading achievement is mediated by student readers' motivation (Guthrie, Wigfield, & You, 2012); teaching readers bears fruit when students are motivated, but has significantly less impact on students' reading development when motivation is lacking. That motivation matters—indeed, that motivation is a prerequisite for students' reading development and reading success—should be a focus of reading instruction:

> As efforts focused primarily on skill building and strategy instruction have continually failed to improve national student performance and narrow academic achievement gaps, some researchers have begun to focus on how children's motivation to read relates to reading comprehension. (Wigfield, Gladstone, & Turci, 2016, p. 192)

Our long-term teaching goals—for students' successful, wide ranging, and independent reading—are achieved as students develop motivation, knowledge of reading, text processing skills and strategies, and personal commitment (Alexander, 2003). Forzani and colleagues (2020) note that readers' cognitive strategies "are recruited, energized, and sustained by motivational processes during reading." It is this notion of strategy use dependent on motivation that helps us better understand the cognition–affect connection and helps us teach readers. Motivation operates not only in the moment of an act of reading, but throughout our students' histories of reading and learning.

Afflerbach and colleagues (2008) described a further relationship between motivation and readers' skill and strategy use:

> Readers are motivated to be skillful because skill affords high levels of performance with little effort, whereas strategic readers are motivated to demonstrate control over reading processes with both ability and effort. When skill and strategy complement each other, they can provide student readers with motivation and self-efficacy from both sources (I am good at this and I can work through the tough spots) and encourage an appreciation of the value of reading. (p. 372)

As students advance through the grades, the texts and tasks that they encounter are of increasing complexity and challenge. Accordingly, a motivation to read should develop correspondingly to provide support for students as they encounter the ever-growing demands of reading. Unfortunately, research finds that motivation to read may decrease as students get older (Jacobs, Lanza, Osgood, Eccles, & Wigfield, 2002). This decrease in motivation is especially pronounced for school reading, along with the value assigned to school subjects and learning (McKenna, Kear, & Ellsworth, 1995; Miyamoto, Murayama, & Lechner, 2020). Thus, many students are in the precarious position of needing an *increasing* motivation to read as they advance from grade to grade, while experiencing a *decreasing* motivation to read: "To master the skills and strategies . . . children must commit time and effort to learn them; thus students must be *motivated* to learn and then utilize them fully" (Wigfield et al., 2016, p. 191).

EXTRINSIC AND INTRINSIC MOTIVATION

Research distinguishes between intrinsic and extrinsic motivation for reading, with intrinsic motivation related to a student's own interests and extrinsic motivation influenced by outside factors, such as rewards and grades (Wigfield et al., 2016). *Extrinsic motivation* can be defined as "an external incentive to engage in a specific activity, especially motivation arising from the expectation of punishment or reward (e.g., completing a disliked chore in exchange for payment)" (*https://dictionary.apa.org/extrinsic-motivation*).

When we reward students for reading in our classrooms—using prizes or presents—we are offering extrinsic motivation. In contrast, *intrinsic motivation* can be defined as "an incentive to engage in a specific activity that derives from pleasure in the activity itself (e.g., a genuine interest in a subject studied) rather than because of any external benefits that might be obtained (e.g., money, course credits)" (*https://dictionary.apa.org/intrinsic-motivation*). When our students read because they associate reading with happiness, feelings of well-being, or their understanding of the practical value of reading, they demonstrate intrinsic motivation.

The distinction between intrinsic and extrinsic motivation is important to understand; we want motivated students, but need to be on the lookout for reading that is too often extrinsically motivated. Reading in the summer book club to earn a ticket to a concert or sporting event and reading to receive praise from the teacher are examples of extrinsic motivation. In contrast, when reading brings fulfillment, students are intrinsically motivated, as is reading done to fulfill personal goals.

Extrinsically motivated students may appear to be intrinsically motivated as they go about the work of the classroom. They follow instructions and complete assigned texts and tasks. However, these extrinsically motivated students read to complete the task and receive praise or a grade, while the intrinsically motivated student reader aims to understand the text. Further, intrinsically motivated students engage with and persist at tasks when meeting challenges. Extrinsic motivation may be driven by external pressure from teachers, parents, and others that compels students to undertake school reading. A key consideration is helping early readers progress from what may be a predominant external motivation pattern to one that is intrinsic, driven by personal interests, agency, and self-efficacy. When students are not progressing from extrinsic to intrinsic motivation to read, the results are often debilitating: such students typically have lower reading achievement (Guthrie & Coddington, 2009). Yang and colleagues (2018) note:

> There appear to be some positive and reinforcing relationships between intrinsic motivation, self-efficacy, and literacy achievement—intrinsic reading motivation leads to more engaged

reading activities that help the student to become a better reader, and he/she is more likely to have a higher reading self-efficacy and better literacy achievement which in turn help the growth of reading motivation. (p. 4)

Teaching readers should focus on maintaining intrinsic motivation for those students who have it and helping students who are extrinsically motivated develop more intrinsic motivation. When we are intrinsically motivated, reading is a consistent feature of the day, inside and outside the classroom. Readers who read of their own volition and who read frequently are often higher-achieving students (Guthrie & Wigfield, 1997). Being intrinsically motivated leads students to read more, and more time spent reading provides more opportunities for practice and mastery of strategies and skills. In fact, Guthrie and Coddington (2009) note: "An extremely widespread research finding is that internal motivations (interest, intrinsic motivation) are positively correlated with reading achievement, and external motivations (pressure, requirements, and rules) are not correlated with reading achievement" (p. 507).

While we strive to instill intrinsic motivation, our students can be interesting mixes of both intrinsic and extrinsic motivation to read. They enthusiastically read science fiction or a blog on skateboarding, demonstrating the immediate usefulness and worth of reading. In contrast, they may procrastinate and avoid reading in science or history because they are not interested in the particular topic; they remember past instances of reading about history and science, and they are not drawn back to the subjects. In these cases, extrinsic motivation to avoid failing or receiving a low test score—or to remain in a teacher's good graces—is operating.

ENGAGEMENT

Engagement is regularly paired with motivation; indeed, it is difficult to think of one without the other. Understanding their relationship helps us best plan as we teach readers. Wigfield and colleagues (2008) note that "engagement in reading is the joint functioning of motivational processes and cognitive strategies during reading comprehension" (p. 171). Reading engagement is the partner of reading motivation, and engagement has both near ("I stuck with this text and made sense of it!") and far ("I love to read, and I am a voracious reader!") outcomes. In fact, Cummins (2015) found that "the negative effects of socioeconomic disadvantage can be 'pushed back' in schools and classrooms where students have access to a rich print environment and become actively engaged with literacy" (p. 231). Certainly, any factor that exerts such power during the here and now of reading and over the history of a student's reading development deserves our attention.

In teaching readers, we want to foster engagement in students' moment-to-moment reading, with effort and attention given to the mesmerizing fairy tale or the information-dense science text. This is engagement as a catalyst of accomplished student reading. We also want our students to return enthusiastically to their reading. We want them to become lifelong readers. This is engagement as a consequence of reading. I note that it is critical to ponder the reverse; lack of engagement can be both a cause and a consequence of lower reading skills, as it is implicated in the "reverse Matthew Effect," in which the less able readers remain that way.

MOTIVATION AND ENGAGEMENT IN THE CLASSROOM

Guthrie (2001) notes that engagement is closely related to the environments that we create in school:

> Teachers create contexts for engagement when they provide real-world connections to reading, meaningful choices about what, when, and how to read, and interesting texts that are familiar, vivid, important, and relevant.

What characterizes classroom contexts that promote motivation and engagement? Reading and related tasks must be situated in students' zones of proximal development (ZPD; Vygotsky, 1978), so that students regularly experience success at their effortful work. When work is too difficult or too easy, we risk losing students to frustration or boredom. It is difficult to be motivated to read texts that are beyond our reach (think of the *broadpoint* paragraph), just as it is for students to read texts that they consider to be too simple. Further, we must plan classroom work that allows students to work from positions of power. The benefits of prior knowledge for content domain learning are well documented; when students also pursue learning goals with extensive prior knowledge, we can assume that, more often than not, engagement and motivation are operating.

Curriculum and instruction should also focus on students' epistemological growth. Students learn that their knowledge matters when they are called on to critique and evaluate the texts they read and the authors that wrote them. The opportunity to show what they know can lead to motivation. When student feedback to peers encourages revision of thinking and writing, students are motivated by knowing that they helped a classmate. And, in turn, classmates can be motivated by knowing that their fellow students are supportive. Finally, providing student choice can influence student achievement and motivation (Schunk & Bursuck, 2016).

The characteristics of classrooms in which student motivation and engagement are encouraged and maintained are well documented (Alexander, 2003; Guthrie, 2008; Horn, 2017; Schiefele & Loweke, 2018). In fact, we have voluminous research and numerous implications to consider. The recent volume, *How People Learn II: Learners, Contexts, and Cultures* (National Academies of Sciences, Engineering, and Medicine, 2018) lists instructional approaches that encourage student readers' motivation and engagement. They include:

- helping students set desired learning goals, as well as goals for performance that are appropriately challenging;
- creating learning experiences that students value;
- supporting students' sense of control and autonomy;
- developing students' sense of competency by helping them to recognize, monitor, and strategize about their learning progress; and
- creating an emotionally supportive and nonthreatening learning environment where learners feel safe and valued[1]

Complementing this focus on classroom environments, Horn (2017) describes the social and emotional aspects of classrooms that support students' motivation and engagement. Emphasizing these factors puts us in position to create instruction that incorporates motivation and engagement as specific goals for teaching readers. She focuses on five supports: students' sense of belongingness; the meaningfulness of learning; and students' competence, accountability, and autonomy.

How do motivation, engagement, and a *sense of belongingness* relate to one another? Horn (2017) proposes that belongingness reflects students'

---

[1] Retrieved from *http://sites.nationalacademies.org/cs/groups/dbassesite/documents/webpage/dbasse_189180.pdf*.

"innate need to establish close relationships with others." When students understand that reading and reading-related tasks in the classroom offer opportunities to develop these close relationships with peers and their teacher, they are motivated to do so and engage in the work of the classroom. Our classroom structures and routines should offer students opportunities to give, receive, and appreciate support: "When students experience frequent, pleasant interactions with others or feel that those around them are concerned for their well-being, they feel like they belong" (Horn, 2017).

A second key to the motivating and engaging classroom is the *meaningfulness of learning*. What qualifies as "meaningfulness?" Answering this question begs a dual view—meaningful from both teaching and learning perspectives—as when teachers plan classroom activities that contribute to student growth in strategies and skills, such as a lesson on comprehension monitoring to improve students' metacognition. However, the adult perspective on meaningfulness does not necessarily transfer to all students. How a comprehension strategy lesson or a comprehension monitoring lesson is imbued with meaningfulness may be immediately obvious to us as teachers, but the value of the lesson and expected learning may be lost on students. In contrast, understanding a text that speaks to students' personal interests may be exceedingly interesting. Thus, a key to establishing meaningfulness from the student's perspective, and in relation to motivation and engagement, depends on students' ability to understand the benefit of what is being taught and learned. When students "get it"—when they understand the value of participating and learning—they are prone to engagement. When the point of a lesson or an assigned reading is not obvious, students may be reluctant to buy into what is offered. Note that disengaged and unmotivated student behavior can be the result of classroom work perceived by students to be "mindless" or of no consequence, or of learning objectives that are too abstract or ill defined. Learning that is demonstrably useful and contributes to classroom engagement and interaction is a core aspect of meaningfulness.

A further influence on motivation and engagement is *students' competence*. Our student readers must experience success, as it allows them to feel competent and to further develop self-efficacy. Self-efficacy is motivating and contributes to engagement. Nothing succeeds like success, and few things motivate like success! Our good teaching thus includes determining accessible texts; related, doable tasks; appropriately scaffolded instruction; and our calling attention to things that our students do well. Horn (2017) also notes that we can encourage our students to gain further competence "by normalizing mistakes as opportunities to grow and learn." Students' risk taking should not result in less engagement. Rather, it should be part of a daily classroom routine and a recognized step in learning.

As students matriculate and mature, they should develop the sense of *accountability*, to themselves and others. In doing so, motivation to do well can fuel students' reading work and engagement with reading results. Classrooms in which students experience the rights and responsibilities of becoming better readers help develop this accountability. Developing pride in one's reading work feeds accountability to one's self as well as others. Finally, students' *autonomy*—in learning from a text and using what is learned—reflects the satisfaction that we receive from work well done. Giving students choices in reading—in terms of texts and reading-related tasks—also contributes to their motivation and engagement.

Schiefele, Schaffner, Möller, and Wigfield (2012) and Schiefele and Loweke (2018) describe additional classroom influences on students' motivation and engagement: self-efficacy, challenge, recognition, curiosity, involvement, importance, grades, social, and choice. Brief characterizations of these influences, which are important to consider as we plan to support students' reading motivation and engagement, are discussed in the following sections. Attention to these diverse influences can inform our teaching readers and how we promote motivation and engagement in our classrooms.

• *Self-efficacy.* Self-efficacy is treated in depth in Chapter 8, and the connection with motivation and engagement is of primary importance. Motivated and engaged students believe they will succeed. Thus, our classrooms must be places where students regularly experience success in reading. These successes range from correct identification of letters, to accurate sound and symbol matching, to reading fluently, to learning new vocabulary, and to literal, inferential, and critical comprehension of texts. An important ingredient here is an array of texts and reading-related tasks that meet students at their current levels of competency. Students' reading success—independently or with our scaffolded instruction in ZPD—provides ongoing support for their narratives of "I can do this."

Given the range of student achievement and related self-efficacies, a classroom library should focus on several areas. First and foremost, there must be texts that each student can read successfully. This promotes the development of self-efficacy, which in turn fosters motivation and engagement. Classroom libraries also should contain texts focused on diverse student interests and backgrounds, inclusive of different genres, and representative of students' cultures. Each of these criteria touches on student familiarity and interest, which also feed motivation and engagement. When students succeed at reading, self-efficacy flourishes. Students develop self-worth as readers and understand their accomplishments. This brings happiness and satisfaction, which encourage motivation and engagement.

• *Challenge.* A healthy challenge is a strong motivator for some students—those who have histories of success with reading. A useful frame for considering the "healthiness" of a student's reading challenges is the ZPD. Where on the scale of challenge does critiquing an author's account of a rainforest or pronouncing a consonant blend lie? The key here is supporting student effort at doable challenges and providing feedback on the meeting of the challenge. Teachable moments result not only in learning strategies and text content, they can also highlight the nature of the challenge, how students approach and meet the challenge, and how they succeed at the challenge. As students' reading becomes more complex, challenge requires students' executive functioning and coordination of resources—including effort, strategies, content knowledge, and attention. Learning to succeed when challenged feeds students' motivation and engagement.

• *Recognition.* What student doesn't crave recognition for success and for a job well done? Our positive reactions and feedback to student work have great value in establishing and maintaining motivation and engagement. Recognition for effort and completed work brings happiness and satisfaction. Likewise, recognition while students are working can boost motivation and engagement for completing the task, however difficult. Students' memory of past praise brings them back to reading and an anticipation of future recognition. As noted previously, our voiced recognition must be related to real student accomplishment. Random praise, for which students cannot find referents, may do more harm than good.

There are several keys to providing recognition of student work that contributes to motivation and engagement. First, students should be able to make the connection between our praise and the work they do. Stating, "Good work," may be well intentioned, but it is vague. Better than "Good work" is "I liked the way you reread when you came to that difficult paragraph." The specificity of our praise should help students reflect on what they are doing well. Second, praise and recognition should not be given if work is not well done. We can always be encouraging, and always be appreciative of student work and effort, even when they do not lead to success. However, if students hear our praise for something that didn't occur, or praise that is unwarranted, they may surmise that we aren't paying attention or that we are not sure of what we are talking about.

• *Curiosity.* Curiosity can be a strong motivator; for some students, it is a key part of their personality. When we reflect on the books and teachers who started and supported us on a path of lifelong learning about an interest or passion, we can appreciate the motivating and engaging power of curiosity. It follows that our classrooms should be rich in books and activities that feed curiosity and support an initial interest in a topic so that curiosity, motivation, and engagement go hand in hand. Instruction should also provide opportunities for student curiosity to feature. Over time, students formulate an understanding that reading can both initiate curiosity in a particular subject—"I just read about rainforests and I can't wait to read more about them"—and sustain that curiosity: "I can't believe how many different frogs, with so many different colors, live in rainforests!" As books, articles, and blogs continually arouse students' curiosity, motivation is developed and sustained.

• *Involvement.* While we don't typically gauge the success of our teaching readers in this manner, the ability for "getting lost in a book" is a clear indication that students are motivated and engaged. Students deepen the association of reading with fulfillment, enjoyment, enlightenment, or escape, and they exhibit involvement. Too often, our students' experiences and involvement are limited. They read in content areas to learn facts, and they read literature to discuss plot and character. And too often, the purpose of the reading is to comprehend and report back on what is learned, as in quizzes, tests, and answers to teachers' questions. When we teach readers, we expand the notion of what is read and why it is read. In addition to providing reading materials that encourage students to enjoy or escape, we must provide the time to do so. And we are perfectly positioned to describe to students how our own reading has served to enrich our lives. These notions of reading in service of enjoyment and of developing insights and appreciation often help build the foundation for motivated and engaged reading outside the classroom.

• *Importance.* Students who assign importance to reading know it as a valuable activity. Reading is motivating when viewed as important to students' lives; it helps them accomplish tasks and achieve diverse goals.

Relevance gives students a reason to initiate and persist with the reading. Units of study that focus on important conceptual themes related to student interests encourage enthusiastic reading over a prolonged period of time, sustaining engagement. Regular encounters with reading and using reading in situations where the importance of reading is prominent lead to increased motivation and engagement.

• *Grades.* Grades for reading are a form of recognition. They certainly have great currency in classrooms and homes as a primary indicator of student achievement. Keep in mind, though, that just as grades are a form of reward for those whose grades are high, they are also a form of punishment for those whose grades are low. High grades are accompanied by recognition and praise, which in turn are associated with feelings of accomplishment and happiness. Good grades cannot help but promote motivation and engagement. In contrast, low grades can engender embarrassment, low self-esteem, and a challenge to self-efficacy, which act against a motivation to read or an engagement with reading. Grades provide us with a strong example of both positive and negative Matthew Effects: when high, they bring a happy recognition to the student reader, and when low, they cause the student reader to associate them with failure. The former calls the successful reader back to reading with motivation, whereas the latter turns the student away from reading with diminished motivation and engagement.

• *Social.* Is reading connected with students' social lives? We know that students are social beings, and some are extremely so! Prior to formal schooling, stories read and listened to become occasions for retelling and for acting out with others. So most students are familiar with reading as a social activity. It is only in school where reading may lose connection to these social roots and become something alien and unfamiliar, the likes of which are not motivating or engaging for them. Linking the social aspects of reading to the reading we do in classrooms can be incredibly motivating for students. Often reading is a solitary act as our students construct meaning from text. The product of reading—what is comprehended and what is understood—is sometimes created and then ignored. The social uses of reading, however, create situations in which students' understandings of text can be revised and updated through social interaction with their classmates and teachers. Book discussions, developing a skit or dramatic piece, and embarking on a collaborative project with students' knowledge gained from reading are social at their core. When reading is perceived as offering opportunities for social interaction with classmates, teachers, and family, students' motivation and engagement follow. When reading assignments and reading-related school projects involve collaboration as well, the social nature of reading becomes front and center for students. Whether discussing a novel, reading in unison, or working together to decode and define a new word, one aspect of school that most students enjoy is spending time with classmates.

• *Choice*. When we ask students to choose what they read or to choose a task related to their reading, we encourage motivation and engagement. We expect that choices reflect students' interests and strengths, and choices encourage the development of self-efficacy and reading confidence. Students who are regularly asked to make choices develop a sense of ownership toward reading and possess increasing self-regulation, motivation, and engagement. Accomplished teachers help create opportunities for students to both choose their reading and the tasks related to reading.

In summary, our knowledge of all of these influences on motivation and engagement and how they impact students' reading development and achievement should inform how we structure our lessons: the texts, tasks, and environments that can foster motivation and engagement. The development of reading motivation and engagement in our classrooms should be viewed from both short- and long-term perspectives. In the short term, students should have daily opportunities to deepen their motivation, engagement, and enthusiasm, and these opportunities should occur across the curriculum. Over the long term, we want consistent experiences as students matriculate to help them further develop and maintain motivation and engagement. We should be wary of situations that may result in a "negative" Matthew Effect, in which motivation and engagement are locked in a downward spiral. Experiences with reading whose outcomes include failure at an academic task, diminished self-efficacy, or ego threat can lead a student to withdraw. When a student is focused on protecting the self from situations anticipated to be negative, motivation and engagement suffer.

Although we know much about classroom environments that support student readers' motivation and engagement, research also describes instruction and classroom environments that may work against motivation and engagement. Students lack motivation and engagement in classrooms where teachers dominate discussions, where teachers ask "known-answer" questions, where teachers are critical of student work, and where teachers do not provide students with adequate think time to answer questions and solve problems. In contrast, students report feeling engaged and motivated with reading when teachers listen carefully, ask students what they need, provide a clear rationale for work, attend to student questions, give encouraging feedback, and recognize challenges that texts and tasks might present to student readers (Reeve & Jang, 2006).

ASSESSING MOTIVATION AND ENGAGEMENT

We are fortunate to have evaluation and assessment tools that help us construct understanding of students' motivation and engagement. It is often the case that our discussions with students and our observations of their work provide valuable real-time information about motivation and engagement or the lack thereof. We can see attention and effort as they are applied by motivated and engaged students. In contrast, we may observe distractedness, frustration, and off-task behaviors when students lack motivation and engagement. Based on discussions and observations of work, we are in a good position to identify students who would benefit from our nuanced understanding of their motivation and engagement, and to "dig deeper" into the specifics of each student's motivation and engagement. There are helpful interviews, surveys, and questionnaires that provide this specificity. Focused on students' interests, values, beliefs, goals, and dispositions, they can help us conduct fine-grained analysis of the state of students' motivation and engagement.

The Motivation to Read Profile—Revised (MRP-R; Malloy, Marinak, Gambrell, & Mazzoni., 2013) consists of a reading survey with Likert-scale items and a conversational interview. The MRP-R is designed to provide useful information about the state of students' reading motivation and the contextual factors that influence that motivation. Using MRP-R results, we can anticipate situations in which student readers will be motivated and engaged and construct classroom environments that promote motivation and engagement. The MRP-R includes 20 items such as:

14. I think spending time reading is _____.
    really boring
    boring
    great
    really great

19. When I read out loud, I am a _____.
    poor reader
    OK reader
    good reader
    very good reader

Also included in the MRP-R are conversational items focused on students' self-concepts as readers and the value students place on reading. These items prompt students to discuss motivation-related factors in reading and include:

"What kind of reader are you?"
"What do you have to do to become a better reader?"
"What kind of books do you like to read?"
"What could teachers do to make reading more enjoyable?"

McKenna et al. (1995) developed a similar assessment form, the Elementary Reading Attitude Survey (ERAS), to examine students' attitudes—from which we may divine information that can be used to create classroom reading situations that promote motivation and engagement. ERAS uses cartoon illustrations to depict attitudes toward different aspects of reading. Students circle particular expressions of Garfield the Cat, representing their feelings related to each question. Questions include:

"How do you feel about spending free time reading a book?"
"How do you feel when the teacher asks you questions about what you read?"

In addition, the Motivation for Online Reading Questionnaire (MORQ; Li et al., 2019) examines students' motivation through 20 items, with 5 items related to each of four dimensions: curiosity (learning more about topics of one's interest for the purpose of enjoyment); value (believing that reading and researching online is both useful and important); self-efficacy (students' beliefs about their ability to read and conduct research successfully online); and self-improvement beliefs (students' beliefs that effort can improve their online reading and researching).

As with assessments of students' metacognition, executive function, and self-efficacy, becoming familiar with the different items and prompts in these assessments can help you choose items that provide the most valuable information. The time needed to administer, score, and analyze the full set of items and prompts for any of the assessments—for each student in your class—may be prohibitive. Thus, finding a subset of items, within or across the assessments, that meets your need to know about motivation and engagement may be the most efficient approach. The use of these items, prompts, and questions should complement what is already known about each student and the information gathered from observing children working and from listening to their discussions.

(CHAPTER REVIEW)

1. Describe the reciprocity of motivation and engagement in students' reading development.

2. Describe how high motivation can help a student excel in reading.

3. Next, describe how low motivation can hinder a student's reading development.

4. Experts claim that student readers should progress from extrinsic to intrinsic motivation. Explain the reasoning behind this claim.

5. One way of thinking about motivation and engagement is this: *Reading strategies and skills + Motivation = Engagement with reading*. Please explain.

(CHAPTER 10)

Attributions and Growth Mindsets

The smallest task, well done,
becomes a miracle of achievement.
—OG MANDINO

In this chapter I focus on how students make sense of their reading experiences, how they create narratives of their own reading development and reading achievement, and how these activities influence their ideas about their control (or lack of control) of reading. I highlight how teaching readers can help our students appreciate the "smallest task, well done," and, most important, how students can take credit for such well done work. We examine the related phenomena of attributions, locus of control, and growth mindsets.

Human beings regularly create accounts of how and why things end up the way they do. In school, we can celebrate our work as teachers when we see our student readers grow and succeed and when we create a lesson that motivates and engages students and results in meaningful learning. Out of school, we can congratulate ourselves for a meal that draws rave reviews from dinner guests or a tennis game well played. We can attribute these positive outcomes to our talents and to our efforts: "I knew that using think-alouds for the class would help uncover the nuts and bolts of that critical reading strategy," "I searched for the best-reviewed recipe and followed it to a T," and "I worked hard on my ground stroke." In contrast, we can explain our performance and outcome in relation to luck ("I'm lucky, and that's why the ball took a good bounce."), innate ability ("I was born to follow a complex recipe!"), or the difficulty of a task ("Modeling strategies is an easy part of teaching.") Throughout our lives, we create narratives that explain how and why things happen, and how things turn out. Central to this narrative are attributions—the perceived causes of our lives' outcomes. We make attributions for all that we do and how well we do it. Further, attributions are our accounts of what (or who) is responsible for the results of our work. This narrative reflects how we see ourselves acting in the world or see the world acting on us. Attribution theory (Weiner, 1986) posits that students regularly create explanations for their performance in school, on a test, for a course project, or in response to a teacher's question. The resulting story of these performances, good or poor, is a causal attribution that influences students' future motivations, behavior, and achievement.

When we teach readers, we are teaching individuals who have created different narratives of their reading development and reading ability. A beneficial narrative maintains particular students' efforts; for other students; a detrimental narrative undermines acts of reading. Consider the following self-account of a successful student reader:

> "I'm pretty successful with my reading. I know that when I work hard and apply effort, my teacher tells me I'm doing well, and I get good scores and grades. I believe in myself as a reader, and I think that I am the main influence on whether I succeed in reading, or not. I tend to think that my reading success (or failure) is tied to the amount of effort I give to my reading and my reading assignments."

In contrast, here is a self-account from a struggling reader:

> "I don't do well with reading. I am in the lowest reading group, and I know that most of the kids in my class score higher than me on the weekly quizzes, end of unit tests, and AYP tests. So, when I think about my school reading, there are lots of times when I get low scores, or I can't answer my teacher's comprehension questions. I don't think that I have much influence on my reading and how it works out. Sometimes what I have to read is too difficult, and I am not sure the teacher likes me. I tend to be unlucky at reading; when I guess at stuff I usually guess wrong. Most days, I don't consider myself a reader—in fact, when it comes to reading, I don't think I can succeed."

Imagine that you are the author of either of these different accounts of reading—and declaring yourself a good or poor reader. These attributions, constructed from past experiences with reading, enable or obstruct particular students' reading progress.

Consider your classroom. There may be students who attribute each and every learning outcome, be it a reading struggle or a reading achievement, to their innate ability, to their effort, to luck, or to the difficulty of the task. Or students may link the level of reading success with how much their teacher likes them. Whatever the attribution, there are influential ideas at work, which may encourage or stifle ongoing student achievement, motivation and engagement, and self-efficacy. Looking across the classroom, we may see enthusiasm, activity, and engagement. We may also observe students who withdraw from work and are disengaged and distracted. Some students rise to a challenge and others retreat. Some give supreme effort, while others call it in. It is human nature to construct an explanation of why we succeed or fail, and students regularly create narratives that provide this explanation. The attributions we make and that our student readers make are powerful—whether or not they are accurate.

If you can imagine thought bubbles over each of the students in your classroom, consider what you might find in terms of the attributions they make for their ongoing success or for their consistent failure. The eager, self-assured student readers are thinking, "This is a hard history chapter, but I know that giving good effort and applying myself will help me succeed." In contrast, the struggling student readers have decidedly different attributions, represented by thoughts such as, "I am so unlucky. I always have to read things that are hard—that I know nothing about—or both." Another student reader thinks, "If my teacher liked me, I would be doing better. I'm struggling—and I wish I had a teacher who did like me," or "Doesn't my teacher know I can't read this chapter?" Worse still, a student may be thinking, "I can't read well because I'm stupid."

In these two groups, some students make an attribution for good reading outcomes to effort—an aspect of reading performance that resides within and is controllable by the student. In contrast, the struggling students attribute their prior and present reading outcomes—and future prospects for reading—to external forces: luck, difficult texts, and the degree to which the teacher "likes" them. When we focus on the reality of the attribution for the student, we can see that one is empowering and that the others are debilitating. When effort is viewed as the engine of success, students are motivated to give effort to succeed. In contrast, when luck, lack of intelligence and ability, or not being liked by the teacher are seen as the cause of their reading performance, students consider reading and the outcomes of their reading as not under their control.

Heider (1958) claimed that most people, including students, are "naïve psychologists." Driving our need to be naïve psychologists is the idea is that we are interested in understanding ourselves and our places in the world. We create explanations of how we become the people we are and the causes of the outcomes of our actions. We are always trying to make sense of everything we do. Doing so involves making attributions; students may ask, "Why are my grades higher than Jean's, but lower than Imani's?", "Why do I always go to the extra reading class?", "Why do I struggle when I read in class?", "Why can't I figure out the right answer?", and "How did I get placed in the high-reader group?" The answers that students construct to these important questions reflect attributions. We are all naïve psychologists! It turns out that the attributions we make can be spot-on accurate or wildly off the mark. However, many students believe these "theories of self," whether they are accurate or inaccurate, and use them to shape their daily lives. In the life of the developing reader, attributions can support reading or work to undermine it. Knowing our students' attributions informs our instruction and helps us teach readers.

ATTRIBUTIONS

For our purposes, *attributions* can be defined as "the interpretive processes by which people make judgments about the causes of their own behavior and the behavior of others" (*www.merriam-webster.com/dictionary/attribution*). In our classrooms, students continually make attributions for their behaviors—why a story is easy or difficult to understand, why a question was answered correctly or incorrectly, and why one is in the high- or low-reading group. Bernard Weiner and Carol Dweck conducted seminal research on the attributions that children and adults make for their performances. Research has identified the different dimensions of attributions: *locus*, *stability*, and *controllability*. *Locus* represents where individuals perceive the attribution to reside, either externally or internally, as the basis for succeeding or failing. Consider third-grade readers who have difficulty comprehending a social studies text. An external attribution could be to the level of challenge of the assigned text or task—that because a text is too hard to comprehend, the accompanying task is not doable given the students' skill set. In contrast, an internal attribution might be ability—students feel they don't have the knowledge, strategies, and skills to understand the text. A second internal attribution can be the amount of effort given. Here, we can see that the locus, or place of an attribution, can directly influence students' reading performance. Struggling students who see the text, task, or teacher as controlling the outcome of reading have little reason to attend and apply effort, because they believe that the determinant of their performance is external. In effect, the fix is in. Contrastingly, students who attribute their success—or lack of understanding—to the degree of effort they give may be in a good position to do better. Focusing on the attribute of effort provides students with a mindset of being in control.

The *stability* dimension represents whether or not an attribution is perceived by the student as fixed or variable. A stable attribute is ability, whereas an unstable (or changeable) attribute is effort. It is here in the arena of fixed or variable attributions that much good work has been done to support student readers. For example, when students attribute their performance to the degree of effort given, they are focused on an internal and variable attribution, and they have the potential to control the factor. Students believe that a mediocre performance might be followed by an outstanding performance if a good or better effort is given: "If I try harder at understanding this story, and if I work hard at not getting distracted, my efforts can lead to better reading." In contrast, the student who attributes reading performance to ability may not choose to apply extra effort in future reading assignments, because ability is seen as a fixed attribute: one is either smart or not smart, and there may be little or nothing a student can do about that.

Attributes also can be classified in relation to their perceived *controllability*, or the degree to which an individual has control over them. Controllable attributions include efforts that are reflected in the amount of studying and the intensity of attention and time devoted to work, whereas uncontrollable attributes include being unlucky and being assigned work that is too difficult. When students make attributions to uncontrollable factors, there is no point in working hard, as the outcome is out of their hands: "It's not worth my effort or attention, because nothing I do will influence the outcome."

Locus of Control

The study of attributions follows from research and theory related to locus of control (Rotter, 1966), which examines how people perceive control over the things they do. Consider this description: "Locus of control is an individual's belief system regarding the causes of his or her experiences and the factors to which that person attributes success or failure" (*www.psychologytoday.com/us/blog/moments-matter/201708/locus-control*). We can see from this definition that locus of control is a close relative of attributions. In education, locus of control typically refers to how students perceive the causes of their academic success or failure in school:

> Whether a student has an internal or external locus of control is thought to have a powerful effect on academic motivation, persistence, and achievement in school. In education, "internals" are considered more likely to work hard in order to learn, progress, and succeed, while "externals" are more likely to believe that working hard is "pointless" because someone or something else is treating them unfairly or holding them back. Students with an external locus of control may also believe that their accomplishments will not be acknowledged or their effort will not result in success. (*www.edglossary.org/locus-of-control*)

In other words, our student readers possess not only knowledge of "how they do" as readers, but also theories that explain "why they do." Consider a fourth-grade student who struggles in reading. He has been in the low-reading group for his entire school career—half his young life. When comparing himself with classmates, he considers why this is so, and develops an explanation for why he is in the low-reading group. There are different explanations to consider, which help illustrate his perception of the locus or place of control. They include:

- The books my teacher gives me are too hard.
- My teacher doesn't like me.
- I'm unlucky when I am assessed.
- I'm stupid and will never be a good reader.

(Note: I use the word *stupid* only because it is a word I have heard struggling readers use to describe themselves.) Each of this student's beliefs reveals a detrimental locus of control over possible attributions for his reading performances. This lack of control makes it both difficult and unlikely that he can envision a means to overcome reading challenges. Once an attribution is set, and the locus of control is uncontrollable, it is hard for many struggling students to see a way around bad luck, their perceived stupidity, or their teacher not liking them.

When students consistently make unhealthy attributions, or they perceive their locus of control as being out of their hands, they may develop a debilitating affliction: learned helplessness. Students who continually make such attributions to external forces may convince themselves that they have no ability to influence their negative reading outcomes. They may suffer from learned helplessness, which occurs "when an individual continuously faces a negative, uncontrollable situation and stops trying to change their circumstances, even when they have the ability to do so" (*www.psychologytoday.com/us/basics/learned-helplessness*). Seligman, Reivich, Jaycox, and Gillham (1995) created a list of characteristics of students who have learned helplessness. As you examine each bulleted point, consider the struggling student readers you know. Each characteristic immediately brings to mind particular students that I've worked with in classrooms and clinics, whose will to persist in trying to become better readers is worn down. These students have the following characteristics:

- Low motivation to learn and diminished aspirations to succeed in school.
- Low outcome expectations; students believe that, no matter what they do in school, the outcome will always be negative (e.g., bad grades). In addition, they believe that they are powerless to prevent or overcome a negative outcome.
- Lack of perceived control over their own behavior and the environmental events; a belief that one's own actions cannot lead to success.
- Lack of confidence in their skills and abilities (low self-efficacy expectations). These children believe that their school difficulties are caused by their own lack of ability and low intelligence, even when they have adequate ability and normal intelligence. They are convinced that they are unable to perform the required actions to achieve a positive outcome.
- They underestimate their performance when they do well in school, attributing success to luck or chance, for example, "I was lucky that this test was easy."
- They generalize from one failure situation or experience to other situations where control is possible. Because they expect failure all

the time, regardless of their real skills and abilities, they underperform all the time.

- They focus on what they cannot do, rather than focusing on their strengths and skills.
- Because they feel incapable of implementing the necessary courses of action, they develop passivity and their school performance deteriorates.

This array of learned helplessness characteristics reminds us that teaching readers means conceptualizing student growth and achievement beyond development in strategies and skills. It means that we must attend to the mental health of our student readers. The characteristics should also inform our focus on different aspects of our students' challenges with reading: their locus of control, the attributions they make, and the nature of their learned helplessness. It is especially important to pay attention to the "learned" in learned helplessness. This helplessness is the result of students' attributions in relation to the classroom environments in which they find themselves. Fortunately, in the case of helplessness, things learned can be unlearned, as we shape instruction and our classroom to address attributions, locus of control, and teaching readers.

ATTRIBUTION TRAINING (OR RETRAINING) AND DEVELOPING POSITIVE MINDSETS

When we determine that a student is making attributions that hinder reading development and achievement, we may consider attribution retraining. This approach to instruction has the goal of changing how students view themselves: "Attributional retraining involves a set of procedures that are designed to restructure an individual's dysfunctional explanations for events to more functional ones" (Struthers & Perry, 1996, p. 172). Research on attributions provides valuable information for understanding their power, their role in reading and learning, and how they develop. Yet, the determination that some students make the "wrong" attribution for the outcomes of their work is but a marker on the path to helping them. What about the students who believe that their reading reflects being unlucky or not smart? What about the students who believe that their teacher doesn't like them or that their reading ability is fixed and low and beyond hope of repairing? Fortunately, attribution retraining can help students question and change the narrative they have constructed for attributing success and failure.

Carol Dweck (2015) portrays this retraining as helping students change their mindsets, with the goal of fostering reading development and achievement: "We found that students' mindsets—how they perceive their abilities—played a key role in their motivation and achievement, and we found that if we changed students' mindsets, we could boost their achievement." Further, Dweck (2015) noted that changing students' explanations of their success or failure can be fostered as students examine their learning processes. Specifically, she observed that "we found that having children focus on the process that leads to learning (like hard work or trying new strategies) could foster a growth mindset and its benefits."

Based on these observations and voluminous research conducted by Dweck and other investigators, we can consider features of classrooms in which students develop productive attributions for their work and mindsets that support learning and reading.

SAMPLING THE SCIENCE

Decades of research describe the powerful influence of attributions and growth mindsets on student learning and achievement. Knowing the attributions our students make, their relative negative and positive influences, and how to address student attributions to improve learning is a key aspect of teaching readers. In this section, I consider the theories and research related to attributions and growth mindsets and their implications for teaching readers.

Researchers have examined the influence of students' attributions on school achievement for nearly half a century. Dweck (1975) observed that children who were encouraged to give more effort—to try harder—increased their persistence at challenging tasks. Chapin and Dyck (1976) worked with middle school struggling readers and examined the influence of attribution retraining on students' reading persistence. Attribution retraining encouraged students to make new attributions for their reading performance. For example, students who consistently attribute reading outcomes to being unlucky, or to the teacher not liking them, or to considering themselves "slow" or "stupid" can clearly benefit from unlearning these attributions. In this study, the retraining encouraged students to establish an internal locus of control for their reading, and they demonstrated heightened persistence in reading, when compared with students who did not receive attribution retraining.

Borkowski, Weyhing, and Carr (1988) determined that providing students with reading strategy instruction and attribution training gave a significant boost to students' reading performance, when compared with students who received only reading strategy instruction. Carr and Borkowski's (1989) examination of attributions and reading strategy instruction found that students improved their reading performance as they increasingly attributed their performance to effort. Thus earlier investigations of students' attributions indicated that focusing on effort, an internal, variable, and controllable attribution, can contribute to students' significantly improved reading performance. Attribution retraining (or training) is all about undoing students' harmful patterns of thinking and replacing them with new understandings of how they can control, and succeed at, reading. A key component of attribution retraining is an emphasis on helping students believe that their efforts contribute to their success (Craske, 1988).

Research providing detailed explanations of the relationship between students' attributions and reading performance continues to this day. For example, Berkeley, Mastropieri, and Scruggs (2011) combined attribution retraining with reading strategy instruction with middle school students. Compared with the control group, the students receiving both retraining and instruction performed significantly better in summarizing text and displayed higher attributions to effort for reading success. This attribution to the internal factor of effort was long lasting. Frijters and colleagues (2018) examined students' attributions in relation to reading strategies and skills and readers' inattention and found that students with adaptive attribution profiles performed better at reading and exhibited lower inattention. The researchers concluded that a detailed understanding of student readers' attributions should inform our reading instruction, and that helping students develop adaptive attributions can support their reading achievement.

Nelson and Manset-Williamson (2006) found that students who participated in explicitly taught self-regulation strategies intervention showed greater gains in making accurate attributions. Kolic-Vehovec (2001) concentrated on metacognitive and attribution training for struggling second-grade readers and examined the influence of training on fluency and reading comprehension. Students showed improvement in reading fluency and comprehension as metacognitive and attribution training improved reading accuracy. Results also indicated that students developed more internal attributions (i.e., effort) for their performance only when they received explicit attribution training. Chan (1996) examined struggling readers and found that a combination of reading strategy training and attributional training increased their frequency of reading strategies, improved reading comprehension test scores, and reduced their attributions of low performance to uncontrollable factors.

Repeatedly, and across decades of research, effort appears as a valuable and beneficial attribution for student readers. However, Dweck (2015) reminds us that it's not the *only* thing: "Students need to try new strategies and seek input from others when they're stuck. They need this repertoire of approaches—not just sheer effort—to learn and improve." Dweck's observation reminds us that a sole instructional focus on students' attributions to effort and related encouragement will take our students only so far in terms of improving their reading. It also illustrates the importance of joining cognitive aspects of reading development (strategies) with affective and conative aspects as we teach readers. Combining an emphasis on effort with teaching and learning a continually widening range of reading strategies signals that we are teaching readers.

Some studies also demonstrate that students' attributions and attribution retraining operate similarly in other school subjects. Okolo (1992) examined the effects of attribution retraining for middle school students in mathematics. Students receiving attribution retraining completed more work than students who did not. Students receiving attribution retraining learned more as well. Okolo determined that as attribution retraining positively influenced students' persistence at math tasks, it also positively influenced achievement.

Dweck (2015) introduced the concepts of growth mindsets and fixed mindsets, noting that students who believe that intelligence can be developed (growth mindset) performed better than students who believed that intelligence is static (fixed mindset). She describes aspects of attributions and mindsets that should be addressed as we teach readers:

> We also need to remember that effort is a means to an end to the goal of learning and improving. Too often nowadays, praise is given to students who are putting forth effort, but *not learning*, in order to make them feel good in the moment: "Great effort! You tried your best!" It's good that the students tried, but it's not good that they're not learning. The growth-mindset approach helps children feel good in the short *and* long terms, by helping them thrive

on challenges and setbacks on their way to learning. When they're stuck, teachers can appreciate their work so far, but add: "Let's talk about what you've tried, and what you can try next." (Dweck, 2015)

So maintaining a balanced focus between effort and the strategies and skills that contribute to learning is critical. I note also that students who do not do well with particular reading tasks, but receive praise may perceive this support as strange. Support always is important, but making sure our praise is targeted on the work students actually do and is related to their actual success is imperative (Johnston, 2004); "empty praise" is just that—words spoken by teachers that don't apply to the student's classroom experience.

Research has also broadened our understanding of the need to reconsider effort as the sole attribution that can account for students' reading success. Although it is important to focus on effort, encouraging students to consider attributions for ability should not be ignored (Weiner, 1986). The focus on ability relates to the emotional surroundings of our student reading. We seek to have students make attributions to effort, because they can take pride in their efforts. However, students also take pride in their ability, and it is possible that, given a choice, some students would prefer to be considered smart rather than hard working. Thus, attribution retraining and key teacher feedback may be focused on both ability and effort. Having students weave ability and effort together in their attribution narrative is a suitable goal.

The decades-long investigation of student attributions for their performance outcomes has several important implications. First, students who make internal attributions for their reading perceive the source and cause of their performance as coming from within. Having this internal locus or place makes it possible for students to control the attribution. Second, within this internal control, students must "see" the attribute as flexible. Even though viewing one's self as smart or intelligent may be a balm for self-esteem, intelligence is most often considered "fixed" and not amenable to change. Weiner (1986) reminded us that students appreciate being considered as "high ability." However, students cannot "give," or call up, more intelligence. In contrast, effort is an attribute that is both internal and variable, and research describes the value of students making attributions to effort as they succeed or struggle. Earlier, I noted that students like to consider themselves as "smart," so feedback that focuses on both effort and ability may further motivate students.

Third, research demonstrates that struggling readers often make debilitating attributions that can, if unchecked, consign them to failure experiences. Fourth, research supports the value of retraining students' attributions. Helping a student progress from external attributions (e.g., I am unlucky; My teacher doesn't like me) to internal attributions (e.g., If I give appropriate effort, I can be successful) is possible through attribution retraining programs. Finally, although it is important to acknowledge and praise students' efforts, this praise should be combined with a focus on the specifics of related student learning.

ATTRIBUTIONS AND MINDSETS IN THE CLASSROOM

Our students continually construct narratives of their classroom experiences. They are not stories we ask them to write; without our prompting, they develop their own accounts of why they succeed or fail. Consider Sean, a student who enters school demonstrably behind his classmates in reading development. From day 1 of the school year, he is aware of status and hierarchy in the classroom—a form of social knowledge. Sean, like many students, makes comparisons between himself and his classmates. He notes that he is a member of the reading group with the most-challenged readers. He observes that classmates in other groups are reading different books and that their reading instruction is different. He struggles with reading. Sean is, unconsciously, creating his own theory of why he is different from most of his classmates and of why he is not always successful in reading. This theory develops as Sean considers the causes of his struggles with reading. He considers that he might be *unlucky*—at being assigned books that are interesting, at answering his teacher's questions, or at being asked to read orally in what he considers a challenging part of the story. Or most of his classmates seem to know a lot about the topics of books they are reading, but he doesn't. A second possible cause of his reading struggles is *task difficulty*. Here, Sean believes that the match between the books he has to read and how well he reads them is not a good one. This theory explains why he fails.

Both luck and task difficulty—Sean's possible explanations for his reading performance—are external attributions. As such, Sean has no sense of control over his reading because luck and task difficulty are beyond his ability to influence them. For Sean, reading in school is regarded as a no-win situation—in part because of his belief that he can do little to change reading outcomes. A third possible external cause is perhaps the most debilitating—Sean doesn't believe he has the ability to succeed as a reader. Self-efficacy theory (Bandura, 2006) reminds us that it is common for people to avoid situations in which they believe they will not succeed. Sean's status as member of the low-reading group and his personal struggles to sound out words, read fluently, and answer what for other students are simple comprehension questions present him with a consistent message—that he doesn't have the ability to read well. Over his school career, Sean increasingly focuses on a single word that he believes explains why he is not reading well—*stupid*. No one has ever used this word to describe him, but it is the explanation for his reading challenges, his most powerful theory of self.

Sean's teacher, Mr. Alexi, understands that teaching readers involves the determination of each students' attributions for success and failure. Mr. Alexi knows that attribution training must ensure that the student can succeed at classroom tasks before using attributions for effort. If Sean were to make a supreme effort and experience failure, it may lead to further strengthening of unhelpful attributions. When students' attributions for their reading are known, Mr. Alexi can support positive and productive attributions and also focus on having students rethink detrimental attributions. In doing so, he is in a position to provide reading instruction and experiences that help to establish or maintain students' positive views of themselves and to change those that are negative. Teaching readers in this case involves both focusing on developing reading strategies and skills and developing healthy attributions. As is the case with motivation and engagement, the influence of high-quality reading instruction on student growth is mediated by attributions.

Mr. Alexi uses six steps in most of his approaches to strategy instruction combined with attribution training (Robertson, 2000), presented in Figure 10.1.

Mr. Alexi knows that Sean's previous teachers have been quick and well intentioned in providing support and praise. He intends to continue this positive approach and to take every opportunity to connect his praise with Sean's effort. This connection depends on support that is continuous and on praise that is strategic and deserved. Prior teachers' encouragements that Sean was developing into a good reader were heartfelt, but were too unspecific for Sean to believe. He had difficulty finding evidence to support his teachers' claims that he was really making progress.

Mr. Alexi believes that the best praise is praise well earned. He creates an environment in which Sean can earn praise, receive directive

- Describe the purpose of the new strategy.
- Describe the important role of effort in attributing outcomes to controllable causes.
- Provide examples and nonexamples of how the strategy works.
- Provide models of positive attributions combined with strategy use (e.g., "I got this one right because I used the strategy and tried hard").
- Have students practice combined strategy-attribution sequence with feedback (e.g., "That's great! You worked hard to use the strategy and got the right answer").
- Have students do independent practice of strategy with continued monitoring and corrective feedback as needed (e.g., "Remember to attribute your outcomes to effort plus these steps").

FIGURE 10.1. Steps for attribution/strategy training. From Robertson, 2000, p. 127, reprinted by permission of SAGE Publications, Inc.

feedback, and grow as a reader. This environment includes texts and tasks with which Sean can experience success and daily opportunities to work with Sean so that small successes can be noted, praised, and connected to his efforts. Mr. Alexi follows the advice given by Willingham (2005):

> Praise should be sincere, meaning that the child has done something praiseworthy. The content of the praise should express congratulations (rather than express a wish of something else the child should do). The target of the praise should be not an attribute of the child, but rather an attribute of the child's behavior. Parents and teachers are familiar with the admonition "criticize the behavior, not the child." For similar reasons, the same applies to praise—praising the child carries the message that the attribute praised is fixed and immutable. Praising the process the child used encourages the child to consider praiseworthy behaviors as under his or her control. (www.aft.org/ae/winter2005-2006/willingham)

Mr. Alexi is, in fact, planning to interrupt Sean's narrative of attributions for performance that is self-defeating. When success is experienced on a regular basis and Mr. Alexi helps connect that success with Sean's efforts, it becomes more difficult for Sean to attribute performance to outside influences. And Mr. Alexi continually makes links between Sean's efforts and the positive outcomes of his reading work. He thinks aloud as he links attribution training with strategy training based on the work of Thomas and Pashley (1982):

> Over the next few weeks, on some mornings, we'll have an activity to start off the day. The purpose will be to learn how to be better workers. We all know it's important to try one's best, but the secret is to know how to say the right things to yourself, especially when you're right in the middle of a difficult job. It's certainly not easy to change how we think, but with practice we can do it. Now let's start an exercise. (Teacher tries an item and models an effort statement such as, "I am going to try this even if it is hard.") I want you to try to think out loud as you go along. Listen to each other's thoughts about how you try your best. (p. 135)

This think-aloud seeks to change the narratives created by struggling readers: it is explicit regarding the hoped-for outcomes as well as the means for change. Mr. Alexi shares and reiterates students' self-statements as students work through learning challenges. Gradually, Sean begins to take credit for some of the good outcomes. Recall that when students attribute their reading performances to luck, to task difficulty, and to whether or not a teacher likes them, they are giving up their right to create a positive narrative story.

ASSESSING ATTRIBUTIONS

Given the powerful influence of students' attributions on reading development and reading achievement, assessments that inform us about the state of attributions and that help us keep track of their changes are essential. A first take on such assessment involves candid discussions with students that help us better understand the nature of their attributions, the locus of control for reading, and any indications of learned helplessness. Discussions can be initiated with the following questions:

- How would you describe yourself as a reader?
- How do you think you are doing in reading (with a particular text)?
- Why do you think you read the way you do?
- Is there something you can do to improve as a reader?
- What is that?
- How will that help you improve?

Next, consider having students think aloud. Recall the previous example of teacher talk and thinking aloud from Thomas and Pashley (1982). The teacher states, "The secret is to know how to say the right things to yourself, especially when you're right in the middle of a difficult job" (p. 135). Just as this teacher is providing a think-aloud narrative of making attributions, we can ask students to do the same. To what do students attribute success or failure as they are reading? Do they give consistent information that describes effortful attempts to read or are they resigned to not doing well? Do their attributions vary from school subject to subject and thus to reading in those different content areas? Assessments should help us construct detailed understandings of our students so that we can help them forego negative and debilitating attributions and adopt positive and helpful attributions. Classroom discussions with students are a first step in this process.

Observing students can tell us much about their attributions. Engaged and motivated students are often those who make internal attributions for effort or ability. In contrast, students who attribute their reading outcomes to luck or task difficulty may not attend to lessons and learning goals. Discouraged students are those who seem "checked out" during reading; those who are continually disinterested in reading instruction may suffer from learned helplessness and the feeling that they are powerless to influence the outcomes of their classroom reading. Our hunches about student attributions, locus of control, and learned helplessness, based on our student conversations and observations, can be complemented with published scales, surveys, and checklists that provide more details about the nature and origin of attributions.

The Causal Dimension Scale (CDS; McAuley, Duncan, & Russell, 1992) offers 10 attributional statements in relation to a student's actual performance. Although the CDS was originally developed for examining students' attributions for performance in physical activities and exercise, it is readily applicable to school phenomena, including reading. Students are asked to think about a specific performance, and then rate, on a scale of 1 to 9, their "impressions of opinions of this cause or causes on your performance" (p. 569). In the example in Figure 10.2, we can investigate students' attributions for the causes of their reading performance that involve critiquing an author's claims and evidence to support an argument, applying knowledge gained through reading to address an environmental problem, determining the main idea of a paragraph, decoding a word, constructing overall understanding of a text, and performing a reading-related task. The language of the prompts can be changed

Instructions: Circle one number for each of the following questions. Is this cause(s) something:

1. That reflects an aspect of yourself	1 2 3 4 5 6 7 8 9	That reflects an aspect of the situation
2. Manageable by you	1 2 3 4 5 6 7 8 9	Not manageable by you
3. Permanent	1 2 3 4 5 6 7 8 9	Temporary
4. You can regulate	1 2 3 4 5 6 7 8 9	You cannot regulate
5. Over which others have control	1 2 3 4 5 6 7 8 9	Over which others have no control
6. Inside of you	1 2 3 4 5 6 7 8 9	Outside of you
7. Stable over time	1 2 3 4 5 6 7 8 9	Variable over time
8. Under the power of other people	1 2 3 4 5 6 7 8 9	Not under the power of other people
9. About you	1 2 3 4 5 6 7 8 9	About others
10. Over which you have power	1 2 3 4 5 6 7 8 9	Over which you have no power
11. Unchangeable	1 2 3 4 5 6 7 8 9	Changeable
12. Other people can regulate	1 2 3 4 5 6 7 8 9	Other people cannot regulate

FIGURE 10.2. Causal Dimension Scale applied to reading. The creators of the CDS note that particular items help us identify the locus (or place) of causality (Items 1, 6, 9), external control (Items 5, 8, 12), stability (Items 3, 7, 11), and personal control (Items 2, 4, 10). Adapted from McAuley et al. (1992, p. 569). Reprinted by permission of SAGE Publications, Inc.

to make it more accessible to students. For example, "Permanent" and "Temporary" (Item 3) might be changed to "You can't change" and "You can change," and "Stable over time" and "Variable over time" (Item 7) can be changed to "Stays the same" and "Changes."

Further investigation of students' attributions and mindsets is possible using the Dweck Mindset Instrument (DMI; Dweck, 2006). The DMI asks students to rate responses to statements that include, "You can learn new things, but you can't really change your basic level of talent," "You can change even your basic intelligence level considerably," and "You have a certain amount of intelligence, and you really can't do much to change it." For each statement, students respond on this 6-point scale:

Strongly agree	Agree	Mostly agree	Mostly disagree	Disagree	Strongly disagree

Again, I note that some statements may prove difficult for younger students to understand, calling into question the usefulness of the DMI for particular students. However, the gist of the statements to which students respond can be reworded. For example, the statement "You can always substantially change how intelligent you are" might be reworded as "You can always change how smart you are."

Our careful observation of students as they work, our discussions with them, and our questions focused on attributions and mindsets should reveal the details of how students view their learning: the locus of control as internal or external to the student, stability as fixed or variable, and controllability as under, or out of, student control. This information places us in a good position to help shape positive attributions and locus of control and to help students unlearn learned helplessness.

(CHAPTER REVIEW)

1. What is an attribution?
2. Choose an external attribution, describe it, and explain how it can influence a student's reading development.
3. Next, do the same for an internal attribution.
4. Describe learned helplessness and explain how it develops.
5. Explain how attribution retraining can help struggling readers succeed.

CHAPTER 11

Epistemology and Epistemic Beliefs

> In a world where critical thinking skills are almost wholly absent,
> repetition effectively leapfrogs the cognitive portion of the brain.
> It helps something get processed as truth.
>
> —LAURA BYNUM

> Facts are stubborn things, and whatever may be our wishes,
> our inclinations, or the dictums of our passions, they cannot
> alter the state of facts and evidence.
>
> —JOHN ADAMS

Every day, our students are confronted with information. They read diverse texts in content-area classes, they see advertisements intended to persuade, they encounter Internet articles with questionable content, and they must make decisions as to the accuracy, usefulness, and truthfulness of what they encounter in texts. These decisions—to include a particular source in a class project, to trust one text over another, and to believe an advertisement and choose to stream a new movie—involve epistemic beliefs. In this chapter, I examine epistemic development and how teaching readers with a focus on epistemics helps our students further develop their agency, their motivations, and their understanding of texts and the world.

Defining *epistemology* and *epistemic beliefs* is a challenging task. When asked what these terms mean (which happens infrequently!), I respond, "It's our knowledge about knowledge—the state of knowledge, how it is created, and what counts as "knowledge." And, "It's how and what we think about knowledge." Epistemology and epistemic beliefs tend not to be well understood. Yet understanding these concepts and their influence on students' reading development and achievement are essential for teaching readers. Fostering our student readers' epistemic knowledge is crucial for their growth as critical 21st-century readers.

Epistemology operates as our students determine that a text is truthful or that it is propaganda. Epistemology helps our students identify misstatements, lies, and falsehoods in texts. Epistemic beliefs assist students as they investigate texts to determine which ones are accurate and reliable. They inform our students' decisions about the trustworthiness of an author or Internet site. While comprehension strategies help readers construct meaning, epistemology helps readers vet the meaning they construct—or choose to avoid particular texts altogether. Epistemic beliefs lead readers to determinations of truthfulness or deceit, usefulness or irrelevance. Thus epistemic beliefs "function as a lens through which a person interprets materials and learning demands, and influence learning and instruction processes" (Rebmann, Schloemer, Berding, Luttenberger, & Paechter, 2015, p. 286).

Epistemic beliefs can ultimately influence what students read and what they believe. As students mature, these beliefs are essential for helping them filter, or screen, the believable from not believable, fact from fiction, and truth from lies. Not only are epistemic beliefs important for the filtering and screening roles they play, they are closely tied to other critical aspects of reading: "Epistemic beliefs impact motivation, achievement, text comprehension, learning strategies, teaching conceptions, and additional constructs" (Berding, Rolf-Wittlake, & Buschenlange, 2017, p. 103). For example, consider the fourth-grade student who is the classroom expert on dinosaurs and who is asked to judge the accuracy of a trade book author's portrayal of a *titanosaurus*. The student may determine that the author's account is sufficient or is lacking in important details. When asked to add to the portrayal of *titanosaurus*, the student contributes knowledge to classroom discussions and to fellow students' understanding. Assuming the role of classroom expert is incredibly motivating for the student reader. Knowing that we can compare our knowledge with the knowledge presented in a text and make judgments about texts equips readers with agency. It changes our very understanding of knowledge. And determining that we know as much as (or more) than a published author contributes mightily to self-efficacy. Further, how our students function in society—how they manipulate knowledge or are manipulated by knowledge—is tied to epistemic development:

> The cognitive and intellectual functioning of an individual is significantly determined by his or her views on what knowledge is

and how it is evaluated and acquired. These individual conceptions of knowledge and knowing determine one's level of epistemological understanding. (Zyluk et al., 2018, p. 130)

How is it that epistemic knowledge and epistemic beliefs—aspects
of reading and reading development that are so powerful—are underrep-
resented or missing in reading instruction programs? How can we have
a positive influence on the development of students' epistemic beliefs,
preparing them to take reasoned stances toward the information they
encounter in texts?

As we go through life and learn, our understandings about knowledge coalesce into epistemic beliefs. For our student readers, "epistemic
beliefs are beliefs about the nature of knowledge and how one comes
to know, and they affect general comprehension, reason, and learning"
(Garrett & Weeks, 2017).

The operating idea here is that particular epistemic beliefs and
stances about knowledge are beneficial and empowering for students as
they adopt critical and evaluative approaches to what they learn from
their reading of texts. Consider this account of reading and learning
for students who have epistemic beliefs that are more fully and less fully
developed:

> Students with sophisticated epistemic beliefs about the source of
> knowledge are likely to hold mastery goals, that is, desire to learn
> for the sake of learning, and therefore take a more active role in
> learning. In contrast, students who believe that their primary role
> is to remember what the teacher says may be less prone to process
> actively that information to create their own understanding of the
> content. (Winberg, Hofverberg, & Lindfors, 2018, p. 296)

As described earlier, epistemology not only influences our reading, but
also our approaches to learning and gaining new knowledge. Students
with less-developed epistemologies run the risk of only receiving—and
not questioning or judging—the information gained from reading. If we
lived in a strictly literal world, such reading might suffice. However, we
live in a world in which the nuanced meanings, covert agendas, and subtexts of what we read must also be understood and scrutinized. A logical
conclusion is that our instruction should "help students develop their
beliefs about knowledge and knowing, that is, their epistemic beliefs,
that in turn are supposed to generate productive approaches to learning"
(Elby, Macrander, & Hammer, 2016, p. 122).

Closely related to epistemic beliefs are epistemic stances. How we (and how our students) regard knowledge influences our interactions with texts:

> Epistemic stance refers to knowledge or belief vis-à-vis some focus of concern, including degrees of certainty or knowledge, degrees of commitment to truth of propositions, and sources of knowledge, among other epistemic qualities. (Ochs, 1996, p. 410)

This description of epistemic stance argues for our commitment to prioritizing epistemology for teaching and learning, even though it is not a consistent focus of current reading instruction. Our "beliefs about knowledge and knowing" regularly influence the attention and the regard we give to what we are reading. We read carefully with texts from trusted authorities, and we take such authors at their word. We are skeptical when we encounter texts, authors, and websites whose reliability is sketchy or variable. We may dismiss offhand texts from sources that are known to produce propaganda. Of course, our attitude depends on the reader's ability to know that a source is sketchy, reliable, or of undetermined origin! These epistemic stances toward texts and authors are influenced and permitted by our individual view of what knowledge "is." When we expect to learn from a text, the value of the information and the nature of knowledge should be consistently evaluated. Further, whether or not we consider particular reading and learning to be worthwhile has a great impact on students' willingness to put effort into reading, to attend to texts' contents, and to participate in classroom activities.

If we return once again to the reading of the *broadpoint* paragraph, you may remember that your epistemic stance was influenced by your prior knowledge—or, more probably, by the lack of prior knowledge. And you may remember that your epistemic stance reflected the inability to critically evaluate the text. Your inclination to investigate the claims made by the author and your decision to trust or to be suspicious of the text were constrained by your lack of related prior knowledge. With the *broadpoint* paragraph, you were in position to receive—and not critique or question—the information in the text. This epistemic stance is similar to stances by students who either (1) lack prior knowledge to question anything in the text being read, or (2) have yet to develop the understanding that reading can involve investigating authors, scrutinizing texts, judging accuracy, and deciding if a text is trustworthy. Thus epistemic stance is a key ingredient in critical reading and higher-order thinking.

Epistemic beliefs influence learning and instruction because they represent the reader's perspective for interpreting text and related learning demands (Berding et al., 2017). Consider the elementary school reader who is focused on coordinating strategy and skill and prior knowledge, happy to understand an entertaining story or a factual account of how snowflakes are formed. This student's epistemic beliefs may include the idea that texts contain information that is unfailingly accurate and that authors are always trustworthy. In contrast, the middle school reader who has learned to "read like a historian" approaches each text with strategies for figuring out if a text is worthy of attention in the first place. The student may be required to answer the questions, "Which account of the Boston Tea Party is more trustworthy?" and "Why?" In fact, students' epistemic beliefs can empower them to read critically or to meekly accept as fact all that is encountered in reading.

We learn that epistemic beliefs can influence comprehension and readers' strategies as well as reading motivation and achievement. We learn that when our student readers possess interpretive authority (Applebee, Langer, Nystrand, & Gamoran, 2003)—including epistemic beliefs that empower them to critically evaluate text contents, author expertise, and the suitability of information in the text for their personal goals—they gain agency and the sense that they are in control of both comprehending texts and determining their value. These gains are earned in addition to the impact of epistemic beliefs on other aspects of reading development, including comprehension, motivation, and learning strategies.

SAMPLING THE SCIENCE

Epistemic beliefs refer to an individual's theory of knowledge and knowing. Most elementary school students are not familiar with this term, and yet the vast majority of students are developing these beliefs as they progress through school. Epistemic beliefs relate to students' ideas about what "counts" as knowledge, about where knowledge is located, and about how knowledge develops (Buehl & Alexander, 2001; Schommer, 1994). Epistemic beliefs also influence how students read, whether they are questioning an author's claims or reading only to establish a literal meaning of a text. Epistemic beliefs are associated with reading development and reading performance (Bruning, Schraw, & Ronning, 1999). They influence students' approaches to learning in the classroom, the stances readers take toward a text, and the cognitive skills and strategies that students use (Lee et al., 2016). For example, readers who believe that texts consist of agreed-upon facts attend to establishing a literal understanding of the text (Bråten, Britt, Strømsø, & Rouet, 2011); there is no need for critical or evaluative reading strategies. In contrast, when readers think of the text as being written by an author with a particular point of view or bias, and with a particular purpose, they may focus on critiquing, questioning, or challenging the text (Goldman, 2018; Bruning et al., 1999). Epistemic beliefs influence students' critical reading, as they make judgments about the accuracy and quality of a text and author bias and trustworthiness (Bråten et al., 2011; National Governors Association Center for Best Practices & Council of Chief State School Officers, 2010).

Kuhn (2000) proposed that epistemic development, starting with a naïve understanding of knowledge and how it is produced, often follows a predictable evolution. From this perspective, younger students are what Kuhn calls "absolutists" who believe that knowledge is certain and that there is an objective truth. Young children believe much of what they are told. They believe that what they read in texts is "true," because why wouldn't it be? Adults wouldn't write misleading texts, sprinkled with falsehoods or hidden agendas, would they? Yet accomplished readers evolve from such an all-encompassing trust in a text to a perspective on knowledge from which they pose healthy and sometimes skeptical questions to both the author and the text.

A major contributor to the development of epistemic beliefs is cognitive disequilibrium (Hofer & Pintrich, 1997), which occurs when our existing knowledge is confronted with conflicting information. This conflict calls attention to itself, and in appropriate learning contexts it can prompt students to examine their knowledge and the nature of the conflicting knowledge and decide what to do about it. If we ask our younger students to distinguish fairy tales from real life or to compare their knowledge of a favorite topic with an author's, we help them query the nature and sources of knowledge. It follows that students should be encouraged to learn to consider the fact that "knowledge," or information in a text may be subjective. Kuhn (2000) posited that an advanced stage of epistemic belief is "evaluativism," which is realized as students identify claims made in a text (and by an author) and then determine if supporting evidence is present to judge the value of what is written. Our students' development from "absolutists" (believing that knowledge is certain and that text contains objective truth) to "evaluatists" (knowing that reading invites judgment of the worth of a text) is essential for accomplished reading.

In addition to determining the truth, trustworthiness, and reliability of a single text, students must also account for the knowledge they encounter in different texts and multimedia. As students matriculate, we often ask them to synthesize information from different sources, and epistemic beliefs play a prominent role in how this information, or knowledge, is vetted, combined, and ultimately accepted and understood. According to Bråten and colleagues (2011), students must read different types of texts and "integrate information across sources to construct a more complete representation of the topic or issue than any single resource can afford" (p. 67).

Epistemic beliefs help readers assign relative value to the different texts and portions of texts that they read. For example, knowing that three accounts of climate change may vary, depending on whether they are presented in a research study in a well-respected science journal, in a political campaign advertisement, or in a neighbor's blog equips the reader with a means to "weight" importance and accuracy. Sources deemed suspect, authoritative, and intentionally misleading can be dealt with accordingly.

A detailed accounting of how a learner's consideration of new and conflicting information contributes to epistemic development is provided by Bendixen and Rule (2004). These authors propose that epistemic change is influenced by three factors: *epistemic doubt, epistemic volition,* and *resolution strategies.* First, epistemic doubt (or "disequilibrium" cited by Hofer and Pintrich, 1997) occurs when a student reads something that conflicts with that student's existing understanding. Consider a widely accepted scientific explanation that conflicts with the student's long-held (and differing) account of a particular phenomenon. Or a student reads an account of history that differs from what she already knows. The resulting dissonance can lead students to question their knowledge and beliefs. Students must possess epistemic volition to address the discrepancy: they must understand that it is acceptable, even desirable, to act on this differential knowledge and establish a new understanding. Then student readers must engage resolution strategies to ultimately reconcile the different accounts or to dismiss one out of hand and fully accept the other. Of course, students must be suitably invested in learning from the texts they are reading to acknowledge doubt, operate with volition, and employ strategies to address and resolve the issue(s). Without this investment, epistemic investigations are not considered worthwhile.

EPISTEMIC KNOWLEDGE AND BELIEFS IN THE CLASSROOM

The expected development of student readers' epistemic beliefs is reflected—although rarely explicitly stated—in reading and literacy standards. From elementary through high school, and with respect to different states and national initiatives, we can infer the knowledge level and the epistemic developmental level necessary for students to do well on the standards. In this section, we examine learning standards, ranging from grades 1 to 12, to help us chart the role that students' epistemic beliefs play in reading. Our examination is intended to help illustrate how elementary school students are expected to focus on constructing literal meanings from text, how middle school students are expected to critique an author's approach to characterization, and how high school students are expected to synthesize an understanding of history from diverse and conflicting texts. This movement from the simple idea that "if it's in print, it must be true," to "I must vet text sources to determine their origin and value" reflects the epistemic growth that we hope to foster when we teach readers, and what students ultimately learn from reading.

I begin with two Common Core State Standards, one focused on stories and the other on texts in general. First let's consider a first-grade standard focused on stories:

CCSS.ELA-LITERACY.RL.1.3
Describe characters, settings, and major events in a story, using key details.

This is a fairly straightforward first-grade standard: It requires that students construct a literal understanding of a story and then provide descriptions based on that understanding. They are not required to critique the story, question characters' motives, or evaluate the author's setting or mood. Attainment of this standard is based on a view of reading that requires explicit reading comprehension and then giving back the information based on that comprehension. Students must provide a literal reporting of what is understood.

Next, consider this second-grade standard:

CCSS.ELA-LITERACY.RL.2.1
Ask and answer such questions as *who, what, where, when, why,* and *how* to demonstrate understanding of key details in a text.

Again, the students' task is to establish a literal understanding of text. Students are not asked to judge the accuracy of the information or identify the purpose of the text or the intent of the author. Reading, comprehending, and then literally reporting on the information learned from the text should enable the student to successfully attain the standard.

In light of these two prior standards—standards that I would characterize as "read, learn by establishing literal understanding, and then give back literal information"—let's examine a different type of state standard, this one from The Texas Essential Knowledge and Skills:

§110.4. English Language Arts and Reading, Grade 2

The student is expected to recognize characteristics of persuasive text, including: stating what the author is trying to persuade the reader to think or do; and distinguishing facts from opinion.

To meet this standard, students must understand that texts are sometimes written to persuade the reader—that there is a subtext of purpose underlying the content that is provided in the written text. The second-grade readers must also know the difference between fact and opinion. The standard requires that students understand that not everything written is a "fact" or true. Students' performance on this standard reflects, in part, their knowledge that authors may be offering opinions that need to be understood and vetted and that texts are not necessarily created to inform but also to persuade. Texts serve different purposes, and authors have different motives. All in all, this is a considerable list of epistemic "must haves" second graders need to succeed at the standard! The standard requires that second-grade readers regard a text as something other than a source of information to be learned, remembered, and shared back. Specifically, the standard focuses on texts as purposefully written by authors (in this case to persuade and inform, as opposed to "just" informing) and on the important distinction between facts and opinions.

As our student readers progress, they typically develop epistemic knowledge that encourages them to understand that there are different text structures and different genres of text, that these genres are often linked with particular purposes, that authors write for purposes that may be stated or hidden, and that it is important to understand the subtexts of what we read. Next consider this fourth-grade Common Core State Standard:

CCSS.ELA-LITERACY.RI.4.8

Explain how an author uses reasons and evidence to support particular points in a text.

This standard requires that students possess the knowledge that authors write texts to make particular claims and arguments. Thus students must know that some texts consist of a claim (or claims), and they must be able to locate and identify the claims (or "points") made in texts and to find related evidence, if any is provided. In addition, students' epistemic development should include the understanding that it is a reader's right (and sometimes obligation) to evaluate an author's claims and that evidence in support of claims should be provided. Epistemic knowledge also helps student readers understand that they should be skeptical of claims made without evidence. If a text contains claims made without evidence (or if the evidence is sketchy or irrelevant to the claim), the entire argument and text may be considered faulty and not worthy of consideration. This process reflects student growth in the ability to value, as well as understand, the author, the text, and the message. Finally, it is within the student reader's rights to interrogate texts, to vet them for fact and opinion and claims and evidence, and to use the results of this process to render judgments about the truthfulness, accuracy, and usefulness of a text. Students' abilities to engage in these literate practices reflect considerable epistemic growth and evolving epistemic stances.

Further epistemic development would be reflected in a student's judging the nature and value of a claim and then critiquing the claim–evidence connection or its value to the evidence itself. This particular ability, afforded by a student's epistemic development and stance, is required by the following standard:

CCSS.ELA-LITERACY.RI.6.8

Trace and evaluate the argument and specific claims in a text, distinguishing claims that are supported by reasons and evidence from claims that are not.

In relation to this standard, student readers not only identify claims and evidence, but must also evaluate the claims. The prior examples of standards illustrate that epistemic development is essential for students' progress in becoming informed, critical readers. Dissecting authors' arguments, judging claim and evidence relationships, and evaluating the quality of texts is expected of students in the later elementary grades, a considerable contrast to the earlier elementary grades when students are "only" tasked with reading to establish a literal understanding of the text.

In addition to using the affordances of epistemic development to critically evaluate a text or author, students must also demonstrate the ability to compare and evaluate related texts. Consider this fourth-grade standard:

CCSS.ELA-LITERACY.RI.4.6

Compare and contrast a firsthand and secondhand account of the same event or topic; describe the differences in focus and the information provided.

Firsthand and secondhand written accounts—of a historic event, a schoolyard incident, a scientific phenomenon, or an occurrence in the neighborhood—often vary. Reading and understanding the differences between the two accounts, developing strategies for comparing them, identifying complementary and similar information, and trying to reconcile differing perspectives (or deem them irreconcilable) are essential. Students are asked to read two accounts of one event and then determine if either account is accurate, is influenced by emotion or memory, or is clearly false or embellished. Students succeeding at this standard would also be comfortable answering questions like, "How can two accounts of the same event differ?", "What biases and influences may be operating in both the firsthand and secondhand accounts I've read?", and "Which written account should I trust?" From this understanding—from this epistemic knowledge—students' reading is empowered to seek the authentic and reliable account. Students know that texts reveal the different knowledge sets, biases, and agendas of the authors who create them. This knowledge allows students to make judgments about the quality and worth of the texts they read.

A final example of how literacy and reading standards reflect the expected development of students' epistemic knowledge is found in the State of California standards for reading in history and social studies for grades 9 through 12:

Historical Research, Evidence, and Point of View

1. Students distinguish valid arguments from fallacious arguments in historical interpretations.
2. Students identify bias and prejudice in historical interpretations.
3. Students evaluate major debates among historians concerning alternative interpretations of the past, including an analysis of authors' use of evidence and the distinctions between sound generalizations and misleading oversimplifications.
4. Students construct and test hypotheses; collect, evaluate, and employ information from multiple primary and secondary sources; and apply it in oral and written presentations.

Consider the breadth and depth of students' work that is required to meet this standard and the significant role that epistemic knowledge plays. Students must be able to identify both valid and questionable arguments. They must be able to identify bias and prejudice in texts, and they must be able to critique both the arguments and the reasoning for them. They are expected to learn to judge the accuracy and value of firsthand and secondhand accounts and to distinguish between "sound generalizations" and "misleading oversimplifications." Our brief excursion across different reading and literacy standards illustrates how we expect student readers to develop and achieve. Any of these standards can be scrutinized for the nature of reader strategies that are needed: either critical and evaluative strategies or discipline-based reading strategies. The evolution of students' epistemic knowledge is interwoven with the strategies. The contrast between the knowledge and strategies needed to meet this standard and the standards considered earlier in the chapter helps us appreciate the expected evolution of students' epistemologies from early elementary school through high school.

A synthesis of the research literature on epistemic knowledge, beliefs, and stances as well as the examination of related literacy standards makes the case for expecting and encouraging students' epistemic development throughout their years in school. Figure 11.1 represents the anticipated movement from student readers' generally naïve understanding of texts, authors, and knowledge to a more comprehensive and sophisticated view, reflecting epistemic development.

Based on the contents of Figure 11.1, we can consider instructional foci as we teach readers and encourage their ongoing epistemic development. In the following section, we examine in some detail students' progress from naïve to more informed and comprehensive understanding of reading, texts, and authors.

Naïve: *If it's in print, it must be true.*
Informed: Texts and their authors can be truthful and accurate; they can also be dishonest, inaccurate, or misleading.

Early in their careers as readers, students tend to believe what a text "says"; the idea that texts and authors can be questioned and challenged has yet to take root. In the primary grades, curricula focus on teaching students the mechanics of reading and on fostering students' literal comprehension of text. That this comprehension has been achieved is demonstrated by students answering literal and low-level inferential questions.

Naïve Understanding	Informed Understanding
If it's in print, it must be true.	Texts and their authors can be truthful and accurate. They can also be dishonest, inaccurate, or misleading.
The purpose of reading is to create a literal understanding of the text.	To fully comprehend a text, one should understand it, as well as the author's purpose for writing it.
All authors are to be trusted, and all texts are truthful.	Authors have agendas and intentions, some of which may be obvious and some of which may be hidden or misrepresented. Some authors are not trustworthy; texts can be truthful, and they can contain lies, half-truths, and misinformation.
Texts portray an objective truth (e.g., whales are mammals).	Texts can present different versions of the same thing (e.g., the Civil War, evolution) that vary in agreement, use of facts, and adherence to truth.
Authors can be taken at their word.	Facts should be distinguished from opinions, and claims in text should be vetted to determine if there is evidence to support the claim, and if the evidence is trustworthy.
As I read, I should not question the information presented, including facts, theses, or positions.	As a knowledgeable individual, I have every right to challenge what I believe to be false or inaccurate.

FIGURE 11.1. Students' epistemic development in reading.

Questions revolve around information and facts stated in informational texts (e.g., What is a mammal?, Who was Harriet Tubman?) and narrative texts (e.g., Why did Bergman write the letter?, How did Regis reach the lean-to?) and often involves memory and recall of information that is "right there" in the text.

However, students need to learn that not all texts contain "true" information, and that understanding the information contained in a text is not all there is to reading. As we teach readers, concentrating on familiar types of texts, which contain material that is familiar to students, can help students develop critical and evaluative strategies. For example, advertisements are a readily available genre for orienting students to text that can be misleading or inaccurate. When students are knowledgeable about the content of advertisements that feature bicycles, streaming games, dancing, and taking care of pets, for example, their experience provides a further store of knowledge with which to investigate the truthfulness and accuracy of texts.

> **Naïve:** *The purpose of reading is to create a literal understanding of the text.*
>
> **Informed:** To fully comprehend a text, one should understand it, as well as the author's purpose for writing it.

Much of early elementary reading instruction prioritizes helping students develop the tools to comprehend a text: phonemic awareness, phonics, fluency, and vocabulary and comprehension. Students' successful use of these strategies and skills results in the literal understanding of a text. Although learning these skills is a watershed achievement in reading development, students' literal understanding can be complemented by expanded understanding of texts and authors.

A foray into related epistemic development should focus on students' knowledge of why authors write texts. When asked, many young students can describe why particular texts are written or why authors create them. For example, consider the following questions:

Question: Why did the author write this silly poem?

Response: To make me laugh!

Question: Why did the author write about taking care of fish in an aquarium?

Response: So I can learn enough to talk my parents into buying an aquarium for my birthday.

Question: Why are there advertisements for video games?

Response: To show us how cool they are and to get us to buy them.

Question: Why does this author argue for year-round schooling?

Response: Because she thinks it will help students learn more.

Each of these questions is answered in a manner that illustrates students' understanding of why texts are written. A helpful progression is to build on this existing knowledge and expand students' understanding of the different purposes of authors and of the texts they write. This approach links author and text to intent, a key epistemic development.

Naïve: *All authors and texts are to be trusted.*

Informed: Authors and texts have agendas and intentions, some of which may be obvious and some of which may be hidden or misrepresented. Some authors and texts are not trustworthy.

A logical extension of students' understanding of why authors write texts is having them examine authors' and texts' agendas and intentions. Having considered purpose—be it to persuade, entertain, inform, or mislead—students can further explore the relationship of text and author to human motives. As we investigate why texts are written and the related agendas and intentions of authors, we help students make connections between the purpose of a text and its contents. Our instruction can highlight how readers can determine the trustworthiness of texts and the honesty of authors and how students can strategically identify the purpose of a text or author and then use appropriate critical reading strategies.

Naïve: *Authors can be taken at their word.*

Informed: Facts should be distinguished from opinions, and claims in a text should be vetted to determine if there is evidence to support the claim and if the evidence is trustworthy.

Helping students understand that texts are not always truthful and that authors should be scrutinized depends, in part, on distinguishing fact from opinion. Using consistent guidelines for doing so, we expect that students will develop the ability to make such distinctions. Students' growth in knowing how to identify fact and opinion can be charted in relation to the following statements:

- "I can distinguish between facts and opinions in a nonfiction text."
- "I can describe the differences between facts and opinions."
- "I can explain how the facts support the author's points in the text."
- "What reasons and facts does the author use?"
- "How do authors use facts to justify their thinking?"
- "Do I agree with the opinions of the author?"
- "Why or why not?"

Recent international assessments of reading and literacy describe a dire situation with respect to students' critical reading abilities. For example, the much-needed skill of distinguishing fact from opinion is lacking in many students:

> Reading is no longer mainly about extracting information; it is about constructing knowledge, thinking critically and making well-founded judgements. Contrast this with the findings from this latest round of PISA, which show that *fewer than 1 in 10 (15 year old) students in OECD countries was able to distinguish between fact and opinion, based on implicit cues pertaining to the content or source of the information.* (Schleicher, 2019, p. 14, italics added)

From the perspective of epistemic development, the inability to understand facts, opinions, and the difference between them is disturbing enough. Even more important, the learning related to distinguishing fact from opinion contributes to students' ability to identify claims and evidence, to critically examine the claims made by authors, and to evaluate the evidence they provide to support these claims. This critical reading ability enables students to evaluate opinion pieces, propaganda, advertisements, and the like. In essence, it brings a sense of control to student readers' lives because it can help them in instances in which texts are trying to manipulate understanding and behavior. Without the ability to distinguish fact from opinion or to identify evidence and claims, student readers are at the mercy of the text, regardless of truth, accuracy, or intent.

Naïve: *Texts portray an objective truth (e.g., Whales are mammals).*
Informed: Texts can present different versions of the same event or phenomena (e.g., the Civil War, evolution) that vary in agreement, use of facts, and adherence to truth.

Many young readers believe that "if it is in print, it is true." Over their careers as readers, we hope that students learn to confront and challenge this belief. Different authors may have different "takes" on reality—events, people, and situations—that are presented in texts and that demand readers' scrutiny. The 21st century is sometimes referred to as the "post-truth" or "alternative facts" era, making it essential that as we teach readers, that we prepare them for success in determining what is truthful and what is intentionally misleading.

An examination of different texts and their structures, authors, claims and evidence, and purposes can help students develop critical reading strategies for identifying differences in texts that are written on the same topic, for reconciling different points of view on the same topic, or for establishing that two or more points of view are not reconcilable.

> **Naïve:** *As I read, I should not question the information presented, including facts, theses, or positions.*
>
> **Informed:** As a knowledgeable individual, I have every right to challenge what I believe to be false or inaccurate and to check on information that may be so.

Knowing that one is allowed—and expected—to read critically is as important as knowing how to read critically. Reading critically, investigating sources, questioning claims, and vetting author and purpose all represent our students' core epistemic growth. In turn, these skills can bolster students' self-esteem, feelings of expertise in a particular domain, and self-perception as accomplished readers. Student readers who are knowledgeable about pets, parkour, or the neighborhood park, for example, should be encouraged to use their knowledge when reading. This acknowledgment can bolster students' self-efficacy and motivation—it is empowering to be an expert—while it contributes to students' critical reading and thinking.

ASSESSING EPISTEMIC DEVELOPMENT

Why do you read? Asking students this question elicits a wide range of responses in most classrooms. Along a continuum of development, we might expect to hear, "To find things out," "To learn about frogs," and "To enjoy a story." These answers reflect a vibrant understanding of one aspect of reading—establishing a literal understanding. As students matriculate through the grades, answers to the question may include, "To compare my experience with the author's," "To add to my understanding of solar systems," and "Because I need to find out the most logical explanation of why my ecosystem project failed." Regardless of our students' ages, asking them why they read provides a window into their view of the nature and value of reading from which we can infer their epistemic development. Of course, following up on the question,

"Why do you read?" will provide more detail on both reading and students' epistemics.

As we teach readers, we expect them to reach milestones in epistemic development, especially in relation to the reading curriculum. These milestones include understanding the different purposes of authors and texts, recognizing authors' intentions, being able to determine fact and opinion, understanding the differences between fact and opinion, identifying claims and evidence while analyzing text, determining if there is suitable evidence to support any claims, judging the accuracy and trustworthiness of a text or author, reconciling differing accounts of the same event in two or more texts, and developing a critical voice when reading in an area of expertise. That students' epistemic development in reading is required (although not often announced!) is well charted by the sample standards provided earlier in this chapter.

Unfortunately, there are precious few assessment resources dedicated to evaluating students' epistemic development in reading. In lieu of specific assessments, existing classroom evaluations that focus on students' understanding of fact and opinion and claim and evidence and the ability to distinguish between them can "stand in" for related epistemic development assessment. One example, which is borrowed from the content areas, is the use of the helpful claim, evidence, and reasoning (CER) structure to assess students' epistemic development related to understanding the claim and evidence relationship. CER is associated with science, and it provides a model and means for students to think about scientific phenomena. Usually paired with a hands-on science curriculum, CER requires that students (1) answer questions by creating a claim, (2) offer evidence in support of the claim, and (3) explain the reasoning they use to link claim and evidence. The CER approach fits well with classroom-based science experiments, but it can also be used in any situations in which claim and evidence are instructional targets. Consider a related assessment rubric provided in Figure 11.2. The rubric allows us to assign scores in relation to the developmental progressions we expect for students who are learning to reason with claim and evidence structures in text. Similar approaches to assessment can be used as we chart epistemic development with fact and opinion classroom tasks. Finally, instruction and assessment related to reading and literacy standards that include foci on epistemics can be modeled after the standards themselves, with student attainment of the standard serving as evidence that instruction fostering epistemic growth is successful.

	3	2	1
Claim—a statement that answers a question	• Accurate claim • Answers the question	• Partially accurate claim • Partially answers the question	• No claim or irrelevant claim made • Does not answer the question
Evidence—data offered in support of the claim	• The evidence is appropriate to support the claim. • There is sufficient and detailed evidence provided. • Evidence is used to explain why competing claims do not work.	• The evidence provides partial support for the claim. • The evidence provided is general and partial. • Does not fully explain how competing claims are not valid.	• No evidence or irrelevant evidence provided to support claim • Does not fully explain how competing claims are not valid
Reasoning—the explanation of how claim and evidence are related	• Reasoning offers strong support for linking evidence to claim.	• Reasoning offers sufficient support for linking evidence to claim.	• Reasoning does not offer support for linking evidence to claim.

FIGURE 11.2. Claim, evidence, and reasoning (CER) rubric.

(CHAPTER REVIEW)

1. Describe *epistemic doubt, epistemic volition, and resolution strategies.* Next, using classroom examples, describe how each factor can contribute to students' epistemic development.

2. Describe how a first grader may be expected to be significantly different from a sixth grader in terms of epistemic development.

3. Give an example of how a student's epistemic stance directly influences that student's reading.

4. How does a student's ability to distinguish fact from opinion represent epistemic knowledge?

5. How does searching for evidence in text to support the author's claims reflect epistemic beliefs?

Conclusions

In the Introduction to this book, I stated:

> It is time to focus on *all* of the factors that influence reading development, to examine their power, to understand their relationships, and to realize their promise in nurturing accomplished and enthusiastic student readers. It is time for teaching readers.

I hope that throughout the chapters I have effectively described—and advocated for—the importance of metacognition, self-efficacy, motivation and engagement, attributions, and epistemic knowledge when we are teaching readers. Each factor influences the acts of reading, each impacts reading development and achievement, and each is more than worthy of our attention.

At the outset, I investigated our own reading of the challenging *broadpoint* paragraph. The brief encounter with this paragraph helped us appreciate the cognitive, affective, and conative elements that are involved in trying to construct meaning. I then examined a century of reading research, noting that teaching readers—and paying attention to the set of complex factors that operates in each of our student readers—has been a consistent but underappreciated theme. Scholars in affiliated fields have long contributed to our understanding of reading and to the sciences of reading.

I provided an overview of key terms, noting that one term may be used to describe different concepts, and different terms may be used to describe the same concept. That there is less than full agreement on how reading and reading-related phenomena are conceptualized demands this attention to definition. I described the research and theorizing behind Matthew Effects and suggested that this powerful model is useful for thinking about student growth or lack of growth in cognitive, affective, and conative areas. I also suggested that zones of proximal development and the gradual release of responsibility are useful models for identifying areas of student growth and for teaching readers.

Next, and in light of the century of inquiry that described the value of teaching readers, I considered how and why contemporary reading instruction is the way it is. I examined testing and its extreme influence on reading instruction. Testing is used as the primary measure of student achievement, teacher effectiveness, curriculum effectiveness, and school quality. Testing frames reading as a cognitive enterprise, and test items are focused on strategies and skills. It is next to impossible to find tests with items measuring self-efficacy, motivation, or metacognition. As such, tests are implicated in every consequential decision made related to the policies and practices of reading instruction—even though they are limited to a cognitive account of reading development.

I then considered the influence of the media on how the public perceives reading instruction. A clear and present bias is reflected in stories that focus on *a* single science of reading and that propose word recognition as the needed medicine for students' reading ailments. Advocating for attention to students' self-efficacy, attributions, or metacognition is difficult when the media assert a single cause of students' reading challenges and then prescribe a single remedy. The difficulty is doubled when the media place blame on teachers, who may be portrayed as ignorant or actively working against best practices.

Related to media influences, I questioned the idea of the single science of reading and that science should be so narrowly conceptualized and sampled. The sciences related to students' reading development and reading achievement are broad. Sampling the broader science demonstrates that it is shortsighted to restrict reading instruction to phonemic awareness, phonics, fluency, vocabulary, and comprehension. Acknowledging, valuing, and using all of the sciences of reading to inform our instruction fosters teaching readers.

The individual chapters on metacognition, executive function and mindfulness, self-efficacy, motivation and engagement, attributions and learned helplessness, and epistemic knowledge illustrated the science that contributes to a nuanced and more instructionally helpful understanding of reading. These individual chapters used reading research to describe each of these factors and how they operate to influence both reading development and reading achievement. Classroom vignettes and instructional approaches were provided to suggest how to address each factor when teaching readers. Finally, suggestions for assessment were offered.

GOING FORWARD

Teaching readers demands new approaches to practice and ongoing research to further explain the powerful interrelationships between the factors that are the focus of teaching readers. To conclude the book, I focus on both.

Research and theory should help us create portraits of students as developing readers, attending to metacognition, executive function and mindfulness, self-efficacy, motivation and engagement, attributions and learned helplessness, and epistemic knowledge, as well as cognitive strategies and skills. Over the next decades, research into all the factors that influence reading development and reading achievement should be supported. We are at a point where research provides meaningful descriptions of the cognitive, affective, and conative influences on reading development. Relatively simple interactions, such as the influence of motivation on achievement and the contribution of metacognition to reading comprehension, have been examined. Beyond this, an important goal is conducting research that best helps us understand the "big picture"—students' accomplishments and challenges in relation to the complex array of influencing factors. Describing the interrelatedness of metacognition, executive function and mindfulness, self-efficacy, motivation and engagement, attributions and learned helplessness, and epistemic knowledge is critical. How do these operate to support one another? How do negative or positive reading experiences influence them? Examining these relationships with cognitive strategy and skill learning is also critical. This more complete accounting of factors influencing reading development places us in a good position to teach readers.

As important as conducting research in the sciences of reading is applying the knowledge gained from that research. I note throughout this book that research related to teaching readers has been conducted over the decades and continues to inform theories of reading and literacy development. Unfortunately, most reading instruction does not reflect this robust knowledge: research and theory are not fully realized in practice. Meanwhile, research and theory continue to contribute new understandings of students' reading development. Such research is contained in publications that focus on recent reading comprehension research (Reading for Understanding Initiative; Pearson et al., 2020), the influences of culture on learning (National Academies of Sciences, Engineering, and Medicine, 2018), and the importance of social and emotional learning (National Commission on Social, Emotional and Academic Development, 2018). Each of these publications includes a focus on research and theory that honor strategy and skill, but that reach beyond these areas and incorporate research from affiliated fields.

Hopefully, such volumes and collections of research can share the bookshelf with the National Reading Panel (NRP) Report (National Institute of Child Health and Human Development, 2000). This report is more than 2 decades old, and it continues to be widely cited as the definitive source for the exclusive instructional focus on the "big five" strategies and skills: phonemic awareness, phonics, fluency, vocabulary, and comprehension. While the NRP Report contains much valuable information, it needs companion volumes inclusive of diverse research and capable of influencing classroom practice. In active areas of science, ongoing research serves to confirm, modify, challenge, or dismiss existing theories and practices. During the past decades there has been consistent research that contributes to our understanding of the evolution of the sciences of reading. We are past due in terms of asking, "Should the NRP Report continue as the single authoritative source, or are there other publications whose contents can have beneficial influence on instruction?" The field will benefit from broadly based accounts of what matters in students' reading development and achievement.

PRACTICE

I trust that this book helps raise questions about much of contemporary reading instruction and convinces you about the value of teaching readers. As teachers, our understanding of the broader science of reading and incorporating this knowledge into the curriculum are work enough. Many of us are vexed with the idea of trying to fit more instruction into our teaching days. How can we attend to our students' self-efficacy, attributions, or epistemic development when our lessons are already full? How can we move from teaching reading to teaching readers?

It is one thing to advocate for teaching readers, it is another to achieve it. We have known for decades that the different cognitive aspects of reading may interact, with both beneficial and deleterious effects. For example, learning and practicing phonics lead to increased speed of decoding, which in turn contributes to increases in reading fluency. In turn, improved fluency facilitates comprehension. Previewing information in content-area reading helps readers establish points of reference that assist in constructing meaning. Successful reading is based, in part, on many such interdependencies; cognitive, affective, and conative factors have similar relationships. I suggest that the development of students' metacognition, self-efficacy, motivation and engagement, attributions, and epistemic knowledge are related, and that this relationship gives us different entry points for addressing them.

Consider metacognitive development. We want our students to develop the ability to begin, work through, and successfully complete acts of reading on their own. This development requires an awareness of how their cognitive skills and strategies contribute to the construction of meaning and of having control over applying the strategies when needed. The value of metacognition for managing reading, including setting and monitoring goals, identifying problems, and fixing them, is immense. However, metacognition has many other potential benefits. With metacognition comes self-awareness, which helps students identify the connection between the effort they give and the results of their work. Understanding this relationship further contributes to our students making accurate attributions for their success. Over time, metacognition also helps build self-efficacy, as students come to understand their role and contribution to reading success and reflect on their past accomplishments. Increased self-efficacy, in turn, contributes to students' motivation to read and their future engagement with reading. Likewise, self-efficacy, motivation and engagement, attributions, and epistemic knowledge all have similar symbiotic relationships with one another and with students' reading success. Such interdependencies and relationships can be found in each of the factors reviewed in Chapters 7 through 11.

What is a suitable entry point for teaching readers in relation to these factors within an already full instructional day? Early in this book, I stated, "The cognitive aspects of reading are well researched, and they are invaluable for student readers' success." Given the central role that strategy and skill play in reading and the omnipresence of strategy and skill lessons in reading programs, what better place to teach readers? By this, I mean that an efficient approach to teaching readers involves situating our attention to metacognition, self-efficacy, attributions, and epistemic knowledge in our existing cognitively focused strategy and skill curriculum.

Metacognition assists readers in monitoring their meaning making. Self-efficacy flows from success at strategy and skill lessons and leads students to future motivation and engagement based on that success. Students who give effort and succeed can learn that they are in charge, that there is the accurate attribution to effort for their work well done. Epistemic knowledge and beliefs are readily addressed as our students read more complex and challenging texts, distinguishing fact from opinion and determining claim–evidence relationships.

As we help students develop the strategies and skills that will serve them throughout their lives as readers, we can connect this learning with the critical areas of metacognition, self-efficacy, motivation and engagement, attributions, and epistemic knowledge. Identifying entry points and introducing and teaching the specific factor is key. Kindergartners learning consonant blends and experiencing success are cultivating a belief-in-self as readers and self-efficacy. Elementary students building their academic vocabularies are also learning that reading helps them with important life issues and are motivated to turn to reading. Middle schoolers regularly checking on the effectiveness of their comprehension strategies are increasing their metacognition.

In conclusion, teaching readers helps us addresses our students' diverse cognitive, affective, and conative needs. Reading instruction has ignored the latter two for too long; strategies and skills learned without the complementary development of motivation and engagement, self-efficacy, and the like will not produce lifelong, successful readers. The keys for teaching readers can be found in research about the sciences of reading, which contributes to our robust and effective instruction. As we teach readers, we focus on metacognition, self-efficacy, motivation and engagement, attributions, and epistemic knowledge. We use these factors to augment strategy and skill instruction and truly prepare students for independent and ongoing success at reading.

(APPENDIX)

Healthy Readers Profile

In this book, I have examined the concept of teaching readers. I have considered the influences of metacognition, motivation and engagement, self-efficacy, attributions, and epistemic knowledge on students' reading development and reading achievement. I am hopeful that its contents help to convince you of the value these influences have for classroom teaching and learning. If that is the case, then how we may go about determining that our students are growing? Chapters 7–11 include a section on assessment and introduce various means for gathering and interpreting information on each of these influencers.

This appendix adds a new tool, the Healthy Readers Profile, which is intended to (1) provide ideas for when, where, and how to gather information related to students' growth; (2) provide a form in which students' behaviors—their accomplishments and needs—can be recorded; and (3) provide a venue for sharing information about each student in relation to metacognition, self-efficacy, motivation and engagement, attributions, and epistemic knowledge.

The information recorded in the Healthy Readers Profile can be used to inform classroom instruction in teaching readers; to alert colleagues to particular students' strengths and needs (especially from academic year to academic year); to communicate the educational importance of each of the included factors for teaching colleagues, administrators, and parents; and to chart student development and share the information with the school community. The information recorded in the Healthy Readers Profile can be used to augment the information found in report cards, test scores, and other indicators of student learning.

Healthy Readers Profile

Metacognition, Self-Awareness, and Mindfulness

Classroom observation:

Listening to student conversations:

Student interview:

Informal assessments:

Formal assessments:

(continued)

From *Teaching Readers (Not Reading): Moving Beyond Skills and Strategies to Reader-Focused Instruction* by Peter Afflerbach. Copyright © 2022 The Guilford Press. Permission to photocopy this material is granted to purchasers of this book for personal use or use with students (see copyright page for details). Purchasers can download an enlarged version of this material (see the box at the end of the table of contents).

Self-Efficacy

Classroom observation:

Listening to student conversations:

Student interview:

Informal assessments:

Formal assessments:

(continued)

Motivation and Engagement

Classroom observation:

Listening to student conversations:

Student interview:

Informal assessments:

Formal assessments:

(continued)

Attributions and Locus of Control

Classroom observation:

Listening to student conversations:

Student interview:

Informal assessments:

Formal assessments:

(continued)

Epistemic Knowledge and Beliefs

Classroom observation:

Listening to student conversations:

Student interview:

Informal assessments:

Formal assessments:

References

Afflerbach, P. (1990). The influence of prior knowledge on expert readers' main idea construction strategies. *Reading Research Quarterly, 25*, 31-46.

Afflerbach, P. (2016). *Handbook of individual differences in reading: Reader, text and context.* Routledge.

Afflerbach, P., Biancarosa, G., Hurt, M., & Pearson, P. D. (2020). Teaching reading for understanding: Synthesis and reflections on the curriculum and instruction portfolio. In P. Pearson, A. Palincsar, G. Biancarosa, & A. Berman (Eds.), *Reaping the rewards of the Reading for Understanding initiative* (pp. 216-250). National Academy of Education.

Afflerbach, P., Cho, B., & Kim, J. (2015). Conceptualizing and assessing higher order thinking in reading. *Theory Into Practice, 54*, 203-212.

Afflerbach, P., Cho, B., Kim, J., Crassas, M., & Doyle, B. (2013). Reading: What else matters besides strategies and skills? *The Reading Teacher, 66*, 12-20.

Afflerbach, P., & Johnston, P. (1984). On the use of verbal reports in reading research. *Journal of Reading Behavior, 16*, 307-322.

Afflerbach, P., Pearson, P. D., & Paris, S. (2008). Clarifying differences between reading skills and reading strategies. *The Reading Teacher, 61*, 364-373.

Alexander, P. A. (2003). The development of expertise: The journey from acclimation to proficiency. *Educational Researcher, 32*, 10-14.

Alexander, L., James, T., & Glaser, R. (1987). *The nation's report card: Improving the assessment of student achievement.* National Academy of Education.

Allington, R. (1977). If they don't read much, how they ever gonna get good? *Journal of Adolescent and Adult Literacy, 21*, 57-61.

Applebee, A. N., Langer, J. A., Nystrand, M., & Gamoran, A. (2003). Discussion-based approaches to developing understanding: Classroom instruction and student performance in middle and high school English. *American Educational Research Journal, 40*, 685-730.

Axtell, C., & Parker, S. (2003). Promoting role breadth self-efficacy through involvement, work redesign and training. *Human Relations, 56*, 113-131.

Baddeley, A., & Hitch, G. (1974). Working memory. In G. Bower (Ed.), *The psychology of learning and motivation: Advances in research and theory* (pp. 47–89). Academic Press.

Baker, L. (1985). How do we know when we don't understand? Standards for evaluating text comprehension. In D. Forrest-Pressley, G. MacKinnon, & T. Waller (Eds.), *Metacognition, cognition, and human performance* (pp. 155–205). Academic Press.

Bandura, A. (1986). *Social foundations of thought and action: A social cognitive view.* Englewood Cliffs, NJ: Prentice Hall.

Bandura, A. (1990). *Multidimensional scales of perceived academic efficacy.* Stanford University Press.

Bandura, A. (1994). Self-efficacy. In V. Ramachaudran (Ed.), *Encyclopedia of human behavior* (4th ed., pp. 71–81). Academic Press.

Bandura, A. (2006). Toward a psychology of human agency. *Perspectives on Psychological Science, 1,* 164–180.

Barling, J., & Beattie, R. (1983). Self-efficacy beliefs and sales performance. *Journal of Organizational Behavior Management, 5,* 41–51.

Bendixen, L., & Rule, D. (2004). An integrative approach to personal epistemology: A guiding model. *Educational Psychologist, 39,* 69–80.

Berding, F., Rolf-Wittlake, K., & Buschenlange, J. (2017). Impact of different levels of epistemic beliefs on learning processes and outcomes in vocational education and training. *World Journal of Education, 7,* 103–144.

Berkeley, S., Mastropieri, M., & Scruggs, T. (2011). Reading comprehension strategy instruction and attribution retraining for secondary students with learning and other mild disabilities. *Journal of Learning Disabilities, 44,* 18–32.

Betts, E. (1940). Reading problems at the intermediate-grade level. *Elementary School Journal, 40,* 737–746.

Borkowski J., & Turner L. (1990). Transsituational characteristics of metacognition. In W. Schneider & F. Weinert (Eds.), *Interactions among aptitudes, strategies, and knowledge in cognitive performance* (pp.159–176). Springer.

Borkowski, J., Weyhing, R., & Carr, M. (1988). Effects of attributional retraining on strategy-based reading comprehension in learning-disabled students. *Journal of Educational Psychology, 80,* 46–53.

Boulware-Gooden, R., Carreker, S., Thornhill, A., & Joshi, R. (2007). Instruction of metacognitive strategies enhances reading comprehension and vocabulary achievement of third-grade students. *The Reading Teacher, 61,* 70–77.

Bourdieu, P. (1999). *On television.* The New Press.

Burden, R. (2012). *Myself as a learner scale.* University of Exeter Cognitive Education Centre.

Bråten, I., Britt, A., Strømsø, H., & Rouet, J-F. (2011). The role of epistemic beliefs in the comprehension of multiple expository texts: Toward an integrated model. *Educational Psychologist, 46,* 48–70.

Brummelman, E., & Dweck, C. S. (2020). Paradoxical effects of praise: A transactional model. In E. Brummelman (Ed.), *Psychological perspectives on praise* (pp. 55–64). Routledge.

Bruning, R., Schraw, G., & Ronning, R. (1999). *Cognitive psychology and instruction.* Merrill.

Buehl, M., & Alexander, P. (2001). Beliefs about academic knowledge. *Educational Psychology Review, 13,* 385-418.

Butkowsky, I., & Willows, D. (1980). Cognitive-motivational characteristics of children varying in reading ability: Evidence for learned helplessness in poor readers. *Journal of Educational Psychology, 72,* 408-422.

Carr, M., & Borkowski, J. (1989). Attributional training and the generalization of reading strategies with underachieving children. *Learning and Individual Differences, 1,* 327-341.

Carroll, J., & Fox, A. (2017). Reading self-efficacy predicts word reading but not comprehension in both girls and boys. *Frontiers in Psychology, 7,* 20-56.

Chan, L. (1996). Combined strategy and attributional training for seventh grade average and poor readers. *Journal of Research in Reading, 19,* 111-127.

Chapin, M., & Dyck, D. G. (1976). Persistence in children's reading behavior as a function of N length and attribution retraining. *Journal of Abnormal Psychology, 85*(5), 511-515.

Connor, C., Phillips, B., Kim, Y., Lonigan, C., Kaschak, M., Crowe, E., . . . Al Otaiba, S. (2018). Examining the efficacy of targeted component interventions on language and literacy for third and fourth graders who are at risk of comprehension difficulties. *Scientific Studies of Reading, 22,* 462-484.

Conradi, K., Jang, B., & McKenna, M. (2014). Motivation terminology in reading research: A conceptual review. *Educational Psychology Review, 26,* 127-164.

Craske, M. (1988). Learned helplessness, self-worth motivation and attribution retraining for primary school children. *British Journal of Educational Psychology, 58,* 152-164.

Cummins, J. (2015). Language differences that influence reading development: Instructional implications of alternative interpretations of the research evidence. In P. Afflerbach (Ed.), *Handbook of individual differences in reading: Reader, text and context* (pp. 223-244). Routledge.

Cunningham, A., & Chen, Y. (2014). Matthew effects: The rich get richer in literacy. In P. Brooks & V. Kempe (Eds.), *Encyclopedia of language development* (p. 473). SAGE.

Cunningham, A., & Stanovich, K. (1998). What reading does for the mind. *Journal of Direct Instruction, 1,* 137-149.

De Landazuri, M. (2015). The development of self-knowledge in Plato's philosophy/ El desarrollo del autoconocimiento en la filosofía de Platón. *Logos: Anales des Seminario de Metafísica, 48,* 123-140.

Dewitz, P., & Graves, M. (2021). The science of reading: Four forces that modified, distorted, or ignored the research finding on reading comprehension. *Reading Research Quarterly, 56,* 131-144.

Dolezal, S., Welsh, L., Pressley, M., & Vincent, M. (2003). How nine third-grade teachers motivate student academic engagement. *Elementary School Journal, 103,* 239-267.

Duke, N. (2000). 3.6 minutes per day: The scarcity of informational texts in first grade. *Reading Research Quarterly, 35,* 202-224.

Dweck, C. (1975). The role of expectations and attributions in the alleviation of learned helplessness. *Journal of Personality and Social Psychology, 31*, 674–685.

Dweck, C. (1986). Motivational processes affecting learning. *American Psychologist, 41*, 1040–1048.

Dweck, C. (2006). Dweck Mindset Instrument. Available at *nationalmentoringresourcecenter.org/index.php/toolkit/item/268-growth-mindset-for-intelligence.html*.

Dweck, C. (2015). Carol Dweck revisits the 'growth mindset'. *Education Week* [online]. Retrieved from *www.edweek.org/leadership/opinion-carol-dweck-revisits-the-growth-mindset/2015/09*.

Eccles, J., & Wigfield A. (2002). Motivational beliefs, values, and goals. *Annual Review of Psychology, 53*, 109–132.

Elby, A., Macrander, C., & Hammer, D. (2016). Epistemic cognition in science. In J. Greene, W. Sandoval, & I. Bråten (Eds.), *Handbook of epistemic cognition* (pp. 113–127). Routledge.

Flavell, J. H. (1976). Metacognitive aspects of problem solving. In L. Resnick (Ed.), *The nature of intelligence* (pp. 231–235). Erlbaum.

Flavell, J., Friedrichs, A., & Hoyt, J. (1970). Developmental changes in memorization processes. *Cognitive Psychology, 1*, 324–340.

Fogarty, M., Clemens, N., Simmons, D., Anderson, L., Davis, J., Smith, A., . . . Oslund, E. (2017). Impact of a technology-mediated reading intervention on adolescents' reading comprehension. *Journal of Research on Educational Effectiveness, 10*, 326–353.

Forzani, E., Leu, D., Li, E., Rhoads, C., Guthrie, J., & McCoach, D. (2020). Characteristics and validity of an instrument for assessing motivations for online reading to learn. *Reading Research Quarterly*.

Frijters, J., Tsujimoto, K., Boada, R., Gottwald, S., Hill, D., Jacobson, L., et al. (2018). Reading-related causal attributions for success and failure: Dynamic links with reading skill. *Reading ResearchQuarterly, 53*, 127–148.

Garner, R., & Kraus, C. (1981–1982). Good and poor comprehender differences in knowing and regulating reading behaviors. *Educational Research Quarterly, 6*, 5–12.

Garner, R., & Reis, R. (1981). Monitoring and resolving comprehension obstacles: An investigation of spontaneous text lookbacks among upper-grade good and poor comprehenders. *Reading Research Quarterly, 16*, 569–582.

Garrett, R., & Weeks, B. (2017). Epistemic beliefs' role in promoting misperceptions and conspiracist ideation. Retrieved from *https://journals.plos.org/plosone/article?id=10.1371/journal.pone.0184733*.

Goldman, S. (2018). Discourse of learning and the learning of discourse. *Discourse Processes, 55*, 434–453.

Goldman, S., Greenleaf, C., Yukhymenko-Lescroart, M., Brown, W., Ko, M., Emig, J., et al. (2019). Explanatory modeling in science through text-based investigation: Testing the efficacy of the Project READI intervention approach. *American Educational Research Journal, 56*, 1148–1216.

Greene, J., & Azevedo, R. (2007). A theoretical review of Winne and Hadwin's model of self-regulated learning: New perspectives and directions. *Review of Educational Research, 77*, 334–372.

Guthrie, J. (2001). Contexts for engagement and motivation in reading. *Reading Online, 4*(8). International Reading Association.

Guthrie, J. (2008). *Reading motivation and engagement in middle and high school: Appraisal and intervention.* Corwin Press.

Guthrie, J., & Coddington, C. (2009). Reading motivation. In K. Wenzel & A. Wigfield (Eds.), *Educational psychology handbook series. Handbook of motivation at school* (pp. 503–525). Taylor & Francis.

Guthrie, J., & Klauda, S. (2014). Effects of classroom practices on reading comprehension, engagement, and motivations for adolescents. *Reading Research Quarterly, 49*, 387–416.

Guthrie, J., & Klauda, S. (2015). Engagement and motivational processes in reading. In P. Afflerbach (Ed.), *Handbook of individual differences in reading: Reader, text and context* (pp. 41–53). New York: Routledge.

Guthrie, J., Klauda, S., & Ho, A. (2013). Modeling the relationships among reading instruction, motivation, engagement, and achievement for adolescents. *Reading Research Quarterly, 48*, 9–26.

Guthrie, J., & Wigfield, A. (1997). *Reading engagement: Motivating readers through integrated instruction.* International Reading Association.

Guthrie, J. T., & Wigfield, A. (2000). Engagement and motivation in reading. In M. Kamil, P. Mosenthal, P. D. Pearson, & R. Barr (Eds.), *Handbook of reading research, Vol. III* (pp. 403–424). Mahwah, NJ: Erlbaum.

Guthrie, J., Wigfield, A., & You, W. (2012). Instructional contexts for engagement and achievement in reading. In S. Christenson, A. Reschly, & C. Wylie (Eds.), *Handbook of research on student engagement* (pp. 601–634). Springer.

Hanford, E. (2018). "Hard Words: Why aren't kids being taught to read?" Retrieved from *https://apmreports.org/episode/2018/09/10/hard-words-why-american-kids-arent-being-taught-to-read.*

Heider, F. (1958). *The Psychology of interpersonal relations.* Wiley.

Henk, W., Marinak, B., & Melnick, B. (2013). Measuring the reader self-perceptions of adolescents: Introducing the RSPS2. *Journal of Adolescent and Adult Literacy, 56*, 311–320.

Henk, W., & Melnick (1995). The reader self-perception scale (RSPS): A new tool for measuring how children feel about themselves as readers. *The Reading Teacher, 48*, 470–482.

Hofer, B., & Pintrich, P. (1997). The development of epistemological theories: Beliefs about knowledge and knowing and their relation to learning. *Review of Educational Research, 67, 1*, 88–140.

Horn, I. (2017). *Motivated: Designing math classrooms where students want to join in.* Heinemann. Retrieved July 9, 2021, from *https://blog.heinemann.com/the-5-features-of-a-motivated-classroom.*

Irvin, J., Meltzer, J., & Dukes, M. (2007). *Taking action on adolescent literacy: An implementation guide for school leaders.* ASCD.

Jacobs, J., Lanza, S., Osgood, D., Eccles, J., & Wigfield A. (2002). Changes in children's self-competence and values: Gender and domain differences across grades one through twelve. *Child Development, 73*, 509-527.

Jiang, H., & Davis, J. (2017). Let's know! Proximal impacts on prekindergarten through Grade 3 students' comprehension-related skills. *Elementary School Journal, 118*, 177-206.

Johnston, P. (2004). *Choice words: How our language affects children's learning.* Stenhouse.

Johnston, P., & Afflerbach, P. (1985). The process of constructing main ideas from text. *Cognition and Instruction, 2*, 207-232.

Jung, J. (2018). Effects of task complexity and working memory capacity on L2 reading comprehension. *System, 74*, 21-37.

Kienhues, D., Ferguson, L., & Stahl, E. (2016). Diverging information and epistemic change. In J. Greene, W. Sandoval, & I. Braten (Eds.), *Handbook of epistemic cognition* (pp. 318-330). New York: Routledge.

Kolic-Vehovec, S. (2001). Self-monitoring and attribution training with poor readers. *Studia Psychologica, 44*, 57-68.

Kuhn, D. (2000). Metacognitive development. *Current Directions in Psychological Science, 9*, 178-181.

Lee, C., Goldman, S., Levine, S., & Magliano, J. (2016). Epistemic reasoning in literary cognition. In J. Green, W. Sandoval, & I. Braten, (Eds), *Handbook of epistemic cognition* (pp. 165-183). Routledge.

Li, E., Gambino, A., Mccoach, D., Rhoads, C., Forzani, E., & Leu, D. (2019). *Psychometric properties of the Motivation for Online Reading Questionnaire (MORQ).*

MacPhee, D., Handsfield, L., & Paugh, P. (2021). Conflict or conversation? Media portrayals of the science of reading. *Reading Research Quarterly, 56*(S1), 145-155.

Malloy, J., Marinak, B., Gambrell, L., & Mazzoni, S. (2013). Assessing motivation to read: The motivation to read profile—revised. *The Reading Teacher, 67*, 273-282.

Markman, E. (1977). Realizing that you don't understand: A preliminary investigation. *Child Development, 48*, 986-992.

McAuley, E., Duncan, T., & Russell, D. (1992). Measuring causal attributions: The Revised Causal Dimensions Scale (CDSII). *Personality and Social Psychology Bulletin, 18*, 566-573.

McCrudden, M. T., Perkins, P. G., Putney, L. G. (2005). Self-efficacy and interest in the use of reading strategies. *Journal of Research in Childhood Education, 20*, 119-131.

McKenna, J., Kear, D., & Ellsworth, R. (1995). Children's attitudes toward reading: A national survey. *Reading Research Quarterly, 30*, 934-956.

Mehan, H., Hubbard, L., & Villanueva, I. (1994). Forming academic identities: Accommodation without assimilation among involuntary minorities. *Anthropology and Education Quarterly, 25*, 91117.

Meltzer, L. (2018). *Executive function in education: From theory to practice* (2nd ed.). Guilford Press.

Millis, B. (2016). *Using metacognition to promote learning.* IDEA Paper #63. IDEA Center.

Miyamoto, A., Murayama, K., & Lechner, C. (2020). The developmental trajectory of intrinsic reading motivation: Measurement invariance, group variations, and implications for reading proficiency. *Contemporary Educational Psychology, 63*, 1–14.

Miyamoto, A., Pfost, M., & Artelt, C. (2019). The relationship between intrinsic motivation and reading comprehension: Mediating effects of reading amount and metacognitive knowledge of strategy use. *Scientific Studies of Reading, 23*, 445–460.

Mokhtari, K., Dimitrov, D. M., & Reichard, C. A. (2018). Revising the Metacognitive Awareness of Reading Strategies Inventory (MARSI) and testing for factorial invariance. Education Faculty Publications and Presentations. Paper 22. *https://doi.org/10.14746/ssllt.2018.8.2.3.*

Moore, J. (1938). The significance of individual differences in relation to reading. *Peabody Journal of Education, 16*, 162–166.

Morgan, P., & Fuchs, D. (2007). Is there a bidirectional relationship between children's reading skills and reading motivation? *Exceptional Children, 73*, 165–183.

Myers, M., & Paris, S. (1978). Children's metacognitive knowledge about reading. *Journal of Educational Psychology, 70*, 680–690.

National Academies of Sciences, Engineering, and Medicine. (2018). *How people learn II: Learners, contexts, and cultures.* National Academies Press.

National Commission on Social, Emotional and Academic Development. (2018). *From a nation at risk to a nation at hope.* Author.

National Governors Association Center for Best Practices & Council of Chief State School Officers (2010). *Common Core Standards for English language arts and literacy in history/social studies, science, and technical subjects.* Authors.

National Institute of Child Health and Human Development. (2000). *Report of the National Reading Panel. Teaching children to read: An evidence-based assessment of the scientific research literature on reading and its implications for reading instruction* (NIH Publication No. 00-4769). Author.

Nelson, J., & Manset-Williamson, G. (2006). The impact of explicit, self-regulatory reading comprehension strategy instruction on the reading-specific self-efficacy, attributions, and affect of students with reading disabilities. *Learning Disability Quarterly, 29*, 213–230.

Ochs, E. (1996). Linguistic resources for socializing humanity. In J. Gumperz & S. Levinson (Eds.), *Rethinking linguistic relativity* (pp. 407–437). Cambridge University Press.

Okolo, C. (1992). The effects of computer-based attribution retraining on the attributions, persistence, and mathematics computation of students with learning disabilities. *Journal of Learning Disabilities, 25*, 327–334.

Pajares, F. (2005). Self-efficacy during childhood and adolescence: Implications for teachers and parents. In F. Pajares & T. Urdan (Eds.), *Self-efficacy beliefs of adolescents* (pp. 339–367). Information Age.

Palincsar, A., & Brown, A. (1984). Reciprocal teaching of comprehension-fostering and comprehension-monitoring activities. *Cognition and Instruction, 1*, 117–175.

Pearson, P. D., McVee, M. B., & Shanahan, L. E. (2019). In the beginning: The historical and conceptual genesis of the gradual release of responsibility. In M. McVee, M. E. Ortlieb, J. Reichenberg, & P. D. Pearson (Eds.), *The gradual release of responsibility in literacy research and practice* (pp.1–21). Emerald Publishing.

Pearson, P., Palincsar, A., Biancarosa, G., & Berman, A. (2020). *Reaping the rewards of the Reading for Understanding initiative.* National Academy of Education.

Peng, P., Barnes, M., Wang, C., Wang, W., Li, S., Swanson, H. L., . . . Tao, S. (2018). A meta-analysis on the relation between reading and working memory. *Psychological Bulletin, 144,* 48–76.

Peura, P., Aro, T., Viholainen, H., Raikkonen, E., Usher, E., Sorvo, R., & Aro, M. (2019). Reading self-efficacy and reading fluency development among primary school children: Does specificity of self-efficacy matter? *Learning and Individual Differences, 73,* 67–78.

Pieschl, S., Stallmann, F., & Bromme, R. (2014). High school students' adaptation of task definitions, goals and plans to task complexity—The impact of epistemic beliefs. *Psihologijske Teme, 23,* 31–52.

Pintrich, P. (2002). The role of metacognitive knowledge in learning, teaching, and assessing. *Theory into Practice, 41,* 219–225.

Pressley, M., & Afflerbach, P. (1995). *Verbal protocols of reading: The nature of constructively responsive reading.* Erlbaum.

Public Broadcasting Service (2019). What parents of dyslexic children are teaching schools about literacy. [*PBS News Hour* video segment]. Retrieved from *https://pbs.org/newshour/show/what-parents-of-dyslexic-children-are-teaching-schools-about-literacy.*

Raudszus, H., Segers, E., & Verhoeven, L. (2018). Lexical quality and executive control predict children's first and second language reading comprehension. *Reading and Writing, 31,* 405–424.

Rebmann, K., Schloemer, L., Berding, F., Luttenberger, S., & Paechter, M. (2015). Pre-service teachers' personal epistemic beliefs and the beliefs they assume their pupils to have. *European Journal of Teacher Education, 38,* 284–299.

Reeve, J., & Jang, H. (2006). What teachers say and do to support students' autonomy during a learning activity. *Journal of Educational Psychology, 98,* 209–218.

Richter, T., & Schmid, S. (2009). Epistemological beliefs and epistemic strategies in self-regulated learning, *Metacognition and Learning, 5,* 47–65.

Robertson, J. (2000). Is attribution training a worthwhile classroom intervention for K-12 students with learning difficulties? *Educational Psychology Review, 12,* 111–134.

Rotter, J. (1966). Generalized expectancies for internal versus external control of reinforcement. *Psychological Monographs: General and Applied, 80,* 1–28.

Schiefele, U., & Loweke, S. (2018). The nature, development, and effects of elementary students' reading motivation profiles. *Reading Research Quarterly, 53,* 405–421.

Schiefele, U., Schaffner, E., Möller, J., & Wigfield, A. (2012). Dimensions of reading motivation and their relation to reading behavior and competence. *Reading Research Quarterly, 47*, 427–463.

Schleicher, A. (2019). *PISA 2018: Insights and interpretations.* OECD.

Schneider, W. (2008). The development of metacognitive knowledge in children and adolescents: Major trends and implications for education. *Mind, Brain, and Education, 2*, 114–121.

Schommer, M. (1994). An emerging conceptualization of epistemological beliefs and their role in learning. In R. Garner & P. A. Alexander (Eds.), *Beliefs about text and instruction with text* (pp. 25–40). Erlbaum.

Schunk, D., & Bursuck, W. (2016). Self-efficacy, agency and volition: Student beliefs and reading motivation. In P. Afflerbach (Ed.), *Handbook of individual differences in reading: Reader, text, and context* (pp. 54–66). Routledge.

Schunk, D., & DiBenedetto, M. (2020). Motivation and social cognitive theory. *Contemporary Educational Psychology, 60*, 361–476.

Schunk, D., & Zimmerman, B. (1997). Developing self-efficacious readers and writers: The role of social and self-regulatory processes. In J. T. Guthrie & A. Wigfield (Eds.), *Reading engagement: Motivating readers through integrated instruction* (pp. 34–50). International Reading Association.

Seligman, M., Reivich, K., Jaycox, L., & Gillham, J. (1995). *The optimistic child.* Houghton Mifflin. Retrieved July 9, 2021, from: *https://numberworksnwords. com/nz/blog/when-children-fail-in-school-understanding-learned-helplessness/#. YOh2qhNKjEY.*

Shell, D. F., Colvin, C., & Bruning, R. H. (1995). Self-efficacy, attribution, and outcome expectancy mechanisms in reading and writing achievement: Grade-level and achievement-level differences. *Journal of Educational Psychology, 87*, 386–398.

Silven, M. (1992). The role of metacognition in reading instruction. *Scandinavian Journal of Educational Research, 36*, 211–221.

Skinner, E., Kindermann, T., & Furrer, C. (2009). A motivational perspective on engagement and disaffection conceptualization and assessment of children's behavioral and emotional participation in academic activities in the classroom. *Educational and Psychological Measurement, 69*, 493–525.

Solheim, O. J. (2011). The impact of self-efficacy and task value on reading comprehension scores in different item formats. *Reading Psychology, 32*, 1–27.

Stewart, J., & Landine, J. (1995). Study skills from a metacognitive perspective. *Guidance & Counselling, 11*, 16–20.

Strang, R. (1961). Controversial programs and procedures in reading. *School Review, 69*, 413–428.

Stanovich, K. E. (1986). Matthew effects in reading: Some consequences of individual differences in the acquisition of literacy. *Reading Research Quarterly, 21*, 360–407.

Struthers, C., & Perry, R. (1996). Attributional style, attributional retraining, and inoculation against motivational deficits. *Social Psychology of Education 1*, 171–187.

Theisen, W. (1920). Provisions for individual differences in the teaching of reading. *Journal of Educational Research, 2,* 560-571.

Thomas, A., & Pashley, B. (1982). Effects of classroom training on LD students' task persistence and attributions. *Learning Disability Quarterly, 5,* 133-144.

Tregaskes, M. R., & Daines, D. (1989). Effects of metacognitive strategies on reading comprehension. *Reading Research and Instruction, 29,* 52-60.

Varga, A. (2017). Metacognitive perspectives on the development of reading comprehension: A classroom study of literary text-talks. *Literacy, 51,* 19-25.

Veenman, M. (2015). Metacognition. In P. Afflerbach (Ed.), *Handbook of individual differences in reading: Reader, text and context* (pp. 26-40). Routledge.

Veenman, M., van Hout-Wolters, B., & Afflerbach, P. (2006). Metacognition and learning: Conceptual and methodological issues. *Metacognition and Learning, 1,* 3-14.

Vygotsky, L. (1978). *Mind in society: The development of higher psychological processes.* Harvard University Press.

Walker, B. (2003). The cultivation of student self-efficacy in reading and writing. *Reading and Writing Quarterly: Overcoming Learning Difficulties, 19,* 173-187.

Weiner, B. (1986). Attribution, emotion, and action. In R. Sorrentino & E. Higgins (Eds.), *Handbook of motivation and cognition: Foundations of social behavior* (pp. 281-312). Guilford Press.

Whitebread, D., Coltman, P., Pasternak, D. P., Sangster, C., Grau, V., Bingham, S., . . ., & Demetriou, D. (2009). The development of two observational tools for assessing metacognition and self-regulated learning in young children. *Metacognition and Learning, 4,* 63-85.

Wigfield, A., & Eccles, J. (2020). 35 years of research on students' subjective task values and motivation: A look back and a look forward. In A. Elliot (Ed.), *Advances in motivation science* (pp. 161-198). Elsevier Academic Press.

Wigfield, A., Gladstone, J., & Turci, L. (2016). Beyond cognition: Reading motivation and reading comprehension. *Child Development Perspectives, 10,* 190-195.

Wigfield, A., Hoa, L., & Klauda, S. (2008). The role of achievement values in the regulation of achievement behaviors. In D. Schunk & B. Zimmerman (Eds.), *Motivation and self-regulated learning: Theory, research, and applications* (pp. 169-195). Erlbaum.

Winberg, T., Hofverberg, A., & Lindfors, M. (2018). Relationships between epistemic beliefs and achievement goals: Developmental trends over grades 5-11. *European Journal of Psychology of Education, 34,* 295-315.

Yang, G., Badri, M., Al Rashedi, A., & Almazrouhi, K. (2018). The role of reading motivation, self-efficacy, and home influence in students' literacy achievement: A preliminary examination of fourth graders in Abu Dhabi. *Large-scale Assessment in Education, 6.*

Ylvisaker, M., & Feeney T. (1998). *Collaborative brain injury intervention: Positive everyday routine.* Singular Publishing.

Zeidner, M., Boekaerts, M., & Pintrich, P. R. (2000). Self-regulation: Directions and challenges for future research. In M. Boekaerts, P. R. Pintrich, & M. Zeidner (Eds.), *Handbook of self-regulation* (pp. 749-768). Academic Press.

Zimmerman, B. (2000). Self-efficacy: An essential motive to learn. *Contemporary Educational Psychology, 25*, 82-91.

Zimmerman, B., Kitsantas, A., & Campillo, M. (2005). Evaluación de la autoeficacia regulatoria: Una perspectiva social cognitiva. *Evaluar, 5*, 1-21.

Zyluk, N., Karper, K., Michta, M., Potok, W., Paluszkiewicz, K., & Urbanski, M. (2018). Assessing levels of epistemological understanding: The Standardized Epistemological Understanding Assessment (SEUA). *Topoi, 37*, 129-141.

Index

Note. *f* following a page number indicates a figure.